FROM IDEA TO MARKET

A COMPLETE GUIDE TO STARTUP VALIDATION

PRIYANKA MADNANI

.

To Headstart Network Foundation, I want to express my heartfelt gratitude for igniting my passion for enabling startup ecosystem and showing me the way to create an impact by helping entrepreneurs in their journey. Everything I have learnt after becoming a #headstarter moulded me to pay back to the society.

To my mentor, college senior and a great friend Mr. Rishabh Kumar Taneja ,thank you for guiding and mentoring me with your experience and knowledege which has been invaluable in shaping my entrepreneurship journey from the day one. This book would not have been possible without your guidance and support.

To Ms. Jasleen Kaur, thank you for refining my words and helping me shape this book. Your kneen eye for detail and commitment to excellence have been instrumental in ensuring the quality of this work.

To my Parents, Mr. Rajesh Madnani and Mrs. Sakshi Madnani, I would be forever grateful for providing me a great education and supporting me always in to follow my passion and persue my dreams. Without you support and hard efforts, i would not be where I am today.

To my husband Mr. Pushpender Khajotiya, thank you for being my constant source of love and support. Thank you for always making my life easier by sharing all my ups and downs in this journey. No matter how many challenges come you have always motivated me to stand and get back in action.

To my younger brother Parth, thank you for always standing by to support me on my journey. Your love, support and encouragement have been an instrument in keeping me motivated and focused on my goals.

To my father-in-law Mr. Madanlal Khajotiya and mother-in law Mrs. Anandi Khajotiya, for all the love, care and support in achieveing my goals and dreams.

To my sister-in-law Jagriti Khajotiya, for all the constant support, love and and understanding. Thank you for being there always.

To my team of Easy To Pitch, for standing with me in all the downs, countinouing the efforts and the dedication towards the organization.

To my friends Anshumaan Singh, Madhu Bansal, Hitessh Saini, Avisha Sharma, Sumedha sarkar and Bikash Sahoo- thank you for being my support system in my journey of growth and entrepreneurship. your encouragement, guidance and companionship made my journey of learning more enjoyable and fullfilling.

This book is dedicated to all of you, who have played a significant role in my life and inspired me to write this book on startup validation. I hope that this book will inspire others to appreciate the value of entrepreneurship and make informed decisions that will benifit them and their loved ones.

With deepest gratitude ,

Priyanka Madnani

Contents

Foreword

" From generating innovative ideas to effectively validating and launching them, Priyanka gives you comprehensive guide to startup validation which equips aspiring entrepreneurs with the tools they need to succeed. With practical insights and actionable strategies, this book is a must-read for anyone looking to perform validation for their ideas to have a successful startup execution ahead."

Hari TN

Co-Founder Artha School of Entrepreneurship| Author| Angel Investor

"Priyanka has been deeply engaged with India's startup ecosystem for more than a decade. Her insights about what makes a startup tick and how to avoid usual pitfalls in the journey are very useful. These will help companies across industries in getting closer to their full potential. In this book she has presented them in a step by step guide format starting with you, the founder, and then giving you the tools to build a healthy and scalable business. It is a must read for all people considering taking a plunge into entrepreneurship."

Arpit Agarwal

Director, Blume Ventures

"I have come across a number of books about start-ups however a book was missing which can start asking basic questions such as 'Are you ready for entrepreneurship?' Priyanka has now authored that book putting together her experience of dealing with budding start-up founders."This comprehensive guide is a must-read for aspiring entrepreneurs, as it offers valuable insights and practical advice on how to turn a business idea into a thriving enterprise. "

Mandar Joshi

Executive ChairmanExecutive Chairman, MStrategy Global , Dubai, United Arab Emirates | Angel Investor | Media Producer | Theatre Actor

"Priyanka's writing style is engaging, and her ability to break down complex concepts into easy-to-understand language makes this book accessible to readers of all backgrounds. Each chapter is carefully crafted to provide actionable steps, real-world examples, and thought-provoking questions, enabling readers to apply the knowledge gained to their own entrepreneurial journey.

What truly sets this book apart is its holistic approach to entrepreneurship, covering everything from market research and validation to building a revenue model and assembling the right team. Additionally, the chapters on organic and inorganic marketing provide valuable tips on how to promote a startup on a budget and reach a wider audience.

I highly recommend this book to anyone considering taking the entrepreneurial leap or looking to refine their existing business strategy. Priyanka's passion for helping others succeed shines through every page, and her book serves as an indispensable roadmap to achieving your entrepreneurial dreams."

Hitessh Saini

Founder and CEO- Fidem.ai | Author| Angel Investor

"If you ever considered owning a business and scaling it you need to learn the dynamics or at least the basics of what you will need. Awareness of what needs to be done and what needs to be avoided can save a lot of time money and energy for you as an entrepreneur. I think this book will help you with just that awareness and basics. Do not try to read through the book in one go. Go one chapter at a time think deeply build your plan. "

Sourabh Goyal

Founder - Successbrew.in | Building People, Brands and Communities | 150k+ Following on Linkedin

"If you're an aspiring entrepreneur or startup founder, Idea to Market is a must-read. Priyanka offers practical insights and actionable strategies for turning your business ideas into a successful startup. Packed with real-world examples and advice, this book is an essential resource for anyone looking to bring their ideas to life."

Harshit Tahiliani

VC Investor @ IvyCap Ventures

Preface

Entrepreneurship is a journey that requires passion, dedication, and an unwavering commitment to making a difference. It is a journey that often begins with a single idea, but requires much more to transform that idea into a thriving business.

In the world of entrepreneurship, ideas are everywhere. From the innovative to the absurd, entrepreneurs are constantly coming up with new and exciting ideas that they believe will change the world. But the truth is that not all ideas are created equal. Some are brilliant and have the potential to transform entire industries, while others are simply impractical or unrealistic.

In today's fast-paced business environment, where competition is fierce and failure rates are high, it's more important than ever for entrepreneurs to validate their ideas before investing time, money, and resources into them. Idea validation is the process of testing and validating an idea to determine whether it is viable, valuable, and worth pursuing.

This book is about the importance of validation in entrepreneurship. It's about understanding that an idea, no matter how brilliant, must be tested and validated before it can be transformed into a successful business. It's about the process of validation, the tools and techniques that entrepreneurs can use to ensure that their ideas are viable and valuable.

The book is divided into several parts, each of which explores a different aspect of idea validation.

Part I provides an introduction to the concept of idea validation, explaining why it's so important for entrepreneurs and outlining the key principles of the process.

Part II delves deeper into the validation process itself, providing a step-by-step guide to testing and validating ideas. The chapter explores the various methods and techniques that entrepreneurs can use to validate their ideas, from customer interviews and surveys to prototyping and testing.

Part III is all about the common pitfalls and challenges that entrepreneurs face when trying to validate their ideas. It explores the most common mistakes that entrepreneurs make, and provides strategies for overcoming these challenges and achieving success.

Part IV features real-world case studies and success stories from entrepreneurs who have successfully validated their ideas and turned them into thriving businesses. These stories offer inspiration and insight into the validation process, and show how entrepreneurs can use the tools and techniques discussed in the book to achieve success.

Whether you're a first-time entrepreneur or a seasoned pro, the lessons in this book will be invaluable. They will help you avoid the pitfalls that so many others have fallen into, and give you the tools and strategies you need to succeed. So if you have an idea that you believe in, but you're not sure how to turn it into a viable business, this book is for you.

The book is based on years of research and experience in the world of entrepreneurship. It draws on the insights of experts and successful entrepreneurs, as well as my own experiences in the field. By providing a comprehensive guide to the idea validation process, the book aims to help entrepreneurs increase their chances of success and avoid the common pitfalls that so often lead to failure.

In conclusion, the importance of validating an idea cannot be overstated in entrepreneurship. In a world where competition is fierce and the cost of failure is high, entrepreneurs must do everything they can to ensure that their ideas are viable and valuable before investing time and resources into them. This book provides a practical guide to startup validation, based on real-world examples and case studies. It's a must-read for anyone who wants to succeed in the world of entrepreneurship and build a successful startup from day zero.

CHAPTER ONE

Are you ready for entrepreneurship?

It seems that everyone has a grand idea for starting a business. Does having an idea, however, actually translate to becoming an entrepreneur? Launching and running a startup business requires hard work, consistency, dedication and a willingness to sacrifice.

Types Of Entrepreneurs

Depending on the styles of entrepreneurship, there are five different types of entrepreneurs. Given below are 5 types of entrepreneurs aAre you ready for entrepreneurship?nd brief explanations for each:

1. Innovator entrepreneurs

Innovator entrepreneurs often think of unique ideas and develop them into profitable ventures. These entrepreneurs usually reshape people's behaviour and actions. Innovators' new and exciting offerings, goods or technology may enable the growth of new markets and allow for new ways of earning a livelihood. These entrepreneurs are typically corporate leaders who make a considerable contribution to the economy.

2. Hustler entrepreneurs

Hustlers generally start with their resources and focus on work rather than raising funds to finance their company. These entrepreneurs concentrate on starting small to grow larger in the future. They are typically self-disciplined and are more likely to handle important situations, from launching their company to marketing their products.

3. Imitator entrepreneurs

These are entrepreneurs who follow in the footsteps of innovative entrepreneurs. Imitators are entrepreneurs who borrow and improve on other people's business ideas. They are constantly searching for ways to improve a product to gain a competitive advantage in the market. Imitators are often a mix of innovators and hustlers.

4. Researcher entrepreneurs

Researcher entrepreneurs are business owners who usually begin a business after they have done extensive research in all related fields. These entrepreneurs typically take a long time to develop goods and decide what is best for their business, since they require a solid foundation in all aspects of the product. They rely more on market research and product development rather than experiments or impulses.

5. Buyers

Buyer entrepreneurs generally find a startup and determine its potential. They often buy it and select the best individual to manage and expand it. These entrepreneurs are usually experts at purchasing businesses that may have a better chance of succeeding.

Entrepreneurs Arise from Diverse Backgrounds

Any field can serve as a springboard for a successful new business enterprise. Entrepreneurs arise from a range of educational, technical, and business experiences that include management, technology, sales and marketing, and scientific research. In addition to an abiding passion to see their innovations realized, entrepreneurs share certain characteristics:

-**They are independent thinkers.**
-**They are optimistic and confident about their chances for success.**
-**They are creative problem solvers.**
-**They are tenacious, visionary, and focused.**
-**They are more likely to act than to wait, and they attack challenges rather than avoid them.**

Are you ready for the journey?

Defining readiness for entrepreneurship can be challenging, as there is no one-size-fits-all answer. However, there are some key traits and characteristics that can be helpful for anyone considering starting their own business. Here are some factors to consider:

1. **Passion and commitment:** Starting a business is a challenging and often stressful process, so it's important to have a deep passion for your idea

and a commitment to seeing it through.

2. **Resilience:** Entrepreneurship is full of ups and downs, so being able to bounce back from setbacks and adapt to change is essential.

3. **Innovation and creativity:** The most successful entrepreneurs are often those who can think outside the box and come up with innovative solutions to problems. Entrepreneurs need to be creative and innovative in order to develop new ideas and solutions. A growth mindset helps them to embrace new ideas, take risks, and think outside the box.

Ultimately, the decision to pursue entrepreneurship depends on individual circumstances and personal goals. However, considering these factors can help to gauge your readiness and increase your chances of success.

There is a very easy mantra that defines how to start a successful entrepreneurial journey!

" Skill-Will-Grill "

Skill

Skills are essential to start and run a successful entrepreneurship venture. Here are some reasons why having the right skills is important:

1. **Problem-Solving Skills:** Entrepreneurs face challenges and obstacles regularly. They need to have strong problem-solving skills to overcome these challenges.

2. **Leadership Skills:** An entrepreneur must be able to lead their team towards success. They should possess strong leadership skills that help them manage their team effectively.

3. **Communication Skills:** Good communication skills are essential for entrepreneurs to communicate their vision, goals, and ideas to stakeholders such as investors, customers, and employees.

4. **Financial Management Skills:** A successful entrepreneur must have a basic understanding of financial management. They should be able to manage budgets, forecast revenue and expenses, and make sound financial

decisions.

5. **Marketing Skills:** Entrepreneurs need to promote their products or services to attract customers. Marketing skills help them to create effective marketing strategies and campaigns.

6. **Time Management Skills:** Entrepreneurs have a lot of responsibilities, and they must be able to manage their time efficiently. Time management skills help them to prioritise tasks and complete them on time.

7. **Networking Skills:** Building relationships with stakeholders such as investors, suppliers, and customers is crucial for the success of an entrepreneurship venture. Networking skills help entrepreneurs to create and maintain these relationships.

In conclusion, having the right skills is crucial for starting and running a successful entrepreneurship venture. It is essential to continuously develop and improve these skills to remain competitive and relevant in the business world.

Will

The will or desire to start a business is a crucial factor in entrepreneurship because it provides the drive and motivation needed to turn an idea into a successful enterprise. Here are some reasons why the will to start a business is important:

1. **Motivation:** Starting a business is a challenging endeavor that requires perseverance, resilience, and a strong work ethic. Without the will to succeed, it can be difficult to overcome the obstacles and setbacks that inevitably arise when launching a new venture.

2. **Vision:** Entrepreneurs need to have a clear vision of what they want to achieve and why. The will to start a business is often driven by a desire to create something new or make a positive impact in the world. Without a strong sense of purpose, it can be difficult to stay focused and motivated during the ups and downs of entrepreneurship.

3. **Risk-taking:** Starting a business involves taking risks, such as investing time, money, and energy into an idea that may or may not succeed. The will to start a business requires a willingness to take calculated risks and step outside of one's comfort zone.

4. **Innovation:** Entrepreneurs are often driven by a desire to innovate and disrupt existing industries. The will to start a business is often fueled by a desire to create something new and different that can solve a problem or

meet a need in a unique way.

Overall, the will to start a business is a crucial ingredient in the recipe for entrepreneurial success. Without it, even the best ideas may never come to fruition.

Grill

While the term "grilling" can sometimes have a negative connotation, it can also be seen as a valuable tool in the entrepreneurship journey. The process of being grilled, or questioned and challenged, can help entrepreneurs to refine their ideas, identify potential weaknesses, and strengthen their business plans.

Entrepreneurship is a challenging journey that requires perseverance, creativity, and adaptability. By being grilled by others, entrepreneurs are forced to think critically about their ideas and plans, which can help them to identify potential pitfalls and develop strategies to overcome them.

Moreover, being grilled can help entrepreneurs to build resilience, as they learn to defend their ideas and respond to feedback and criticism. This can be particularly important in the early stages of a startup, when the entrepreneur may need to pitch their idea to investors, potential partners, or customers.

In short, while being grilled may be uncomfortable, it can also be a valuable learning experience that helps entrepreneurs to refine their ideas and build the skills they need to succeed in the world of entrepreneurship.

Why startup?

Startups opens the door not to a to-do list but rather to new possibilities and challenges that will let you grow with it. Let's jump to the main reasons to join a startup.

1. Flexible schedule: For sure, you'll have a lot of work to do, but you can schedule the tasks according to your own comfort. You just need to negotiate it with your boss. One more advantage is that you can work remotely from any part of the world. The only thing you need is a good Internet connection.

2. Variety of tasks: The opportunities and challenges you will face during your work in a startup will constantly change. This means that you will have a chance to adapt to the situation and master new skills to do the tasks needed for the further development of the project.

3. Creative environment: It's widely known that people who take risks and start new businesses have a lot of ideas and welcome creativity. They explore new approaches, products, and services to be original. That's why you should contact the founders who will help you see everything from a new perspective.

4. Professional growth: Working in a startup from the very beginning enables you to build a foundation of necessary skills and knowledge, gain experiences in different functional areas, and take responsibility for multiple tasks. Besides, as a business grows, you will grow as a professional by obtaining new career opportunities.

5. Friendly team: Since the majority of startups are small, you'll have the chance to get acquainted with all your colleagues personally. You'll also share your ideas and thoughts with your team to boost the company's success. Joining a startup is like becoming a part of a family.

6. Career opportunities: Sometimes a large company pays more than a startup can afford. However, in a startup, you can obtain new incentives and skills while doing completely different tasks. In the long run, you'll have irreplaceable experience as a professional.

7. Generate Employment: Employment is an important factor in the development of any economy. A low employment rate indicates the poor health of an economy. An economy needs to generate more jobs and wage opportunities to accelerate growth. It plays an important role in job creation. The bigger the enterprise, the more job and salary opportunities are created. Therefore, the need for entrepreneurship in India becomes important for economic development.

Mindset plays a vital role

Having the right mindset is crucial for anyone who wants to become an entrepreneur. A positive and proactive mindset is essential for entrepreneurial success.

Entrepreneurs face a lot of challenges, setbacks, and failures along the way. A positive and growth-oriented mindset helps them bounce back from these setbacks and stay focused on their goals.

Having a **"no quit"** attitude is important for anyone pursuing entrepreneurship. Starting a business is a challenging and often unpredictable journey that requires perseverance, determination, and resilience. Here are a few reasons why having a "no quit" attitude is so important:

1. **Overcoming obstacles:** Starting a business often involves facing numerous obstacles and setbacks, such as funding issues, product development challenges, and marketing difficulties. Having a "no quit" attitude means that you are willing to persist through these obstacles and find creative solutions to overcome them.

2. **Staying focused:** Starting a business requires a lot of time and effort, and it's easy to get distracted or discouraged along the way. Having a "no quit" attitude means that you remain focused on your goals and stay committed to your vision, even when things get tough.

3. **Building resilience**: Entrepreneurship can be a rollercoaster ride of highs and lows, and it's important to have the resilience to weather those ups and downs. Having a "no quit" attitude means that you are willing to learn from failures and setbacks, and use those experiences to grow and improve.

Ultimately, having a "no quit" attitude is essential for anyone pursuing entrepreneurship. While starting a business can be challenging, it can also be incredibly rewarding, and those who are willing to persist and persevere are more likely to succeed in the long run.

In conclusion, having a growth mindset and no quit attitude are essential for anyone who wants to become an entrepreneur. It helps them to overcome challenges, be creative and innovative, solve problems, adapt to change, and be effective leaders.

CHAPTER TWO

Market Research and Analytics

Market research is the process of gathering, analyzing, and interpreting information about a specific market, including its customers, competitors, and industry trends. It is important before working on any idea because it helps you identify and understand your target audience, their needs, preferences, and behaviours. Without market research, you may end up investing time and money into an idea that is not well-suited for your target market, leading to a product or service that fails to meet customer needs and generate revenue.

Here are some of the reasons why market research is important before starting a business:

1. **Understanding the market:** Market research helps you understand the market, including your potential customers, competitors, and industry trends. This knowledge can help you develop a business plan that is more likely to succeed.

2. **Identifying opportunities:** Market research can help you identify gaps in the market that your business can fill. This information can help you develop products or services that meet the needs of your potential customers.

3. **Determining demand:** Market research can help you determine the demand for your products or services. This information can help you forecast sales and develop pricing strategies.

4. **Reducing risk:** Market research can help you reduce the risk of starting a business. By understanding the market and your potential customers, you can make informed decisions that reduce the likelihood of failure.

5. **Improving marketing efforts:** Market research can help you develop effective marketing strategies that target your ideal customer. By understanding your customers' needs and preferences, you can create marketing messages that resonate with them.

Market research also helps you make informed decisions about your business strategy by providing insights into the following areas:

- **Product development:** Market research helps you understand what your customers want and need in a product or service, so you can develop a product that meets those needs.

- **Marketing and advertising**: Market research helps you identify the most effective channels to reach your target audience and develop messaging that resonates with them.

- **Pricing strategy:** Market research helps you understand what price points are acceptable to your target audience, so you can set a price that is competitive and profitable.

- **Competition:** Market research helps you understand your competitors and their strengths and weaknesses, so you can differentiate your product or service and develop a unique selling proposition.

In summary, market research is critical to the success of any startup. It helps you understand the market, identify opportunities, determine demand, reduce risk, and improve marketing efforts. By conducting thorough market research, you can increase your chances of success and create a strong foundation for your business

There are several types of market research:

1. **Exploratory Research:** This type of research is conducted to gather preliminary information about the market, customers, and competitors. It helps in identifying the research problem and defining the research objectives.

2. **Descriptive Research:** This research is used to describe the characteristics of a particular market, such as size, growth rate, demographics, and consumer behavior.

3. **Causal Research:** This research is used to determine the cause-and-effect relationship between variables. It helps in understanding how changes in one variable affect another variable.

4. **Quantitative Research:** This research involves collecting and analyzing numerical data through surveys, experiments, and statistical analysis. It helps in quantifying the market and customer preferences.

5. **Qualitative Research:** This research involves collecting non-numerical data through focus groups, interviews, and observation. It helps in understanding customer perceptions, attitudes, and behavior.

6. **Primary Research:** This research involves collecting new data directly from the market through surveys, interviews, and observation.

7. **Secondary Research:** This research involves collecting existing data from sources such as industry reports, government statistics, and online databases.

By using different types of market research, businesses can gain a better understanding of their target market and make more informed decisions about their products and services.

Steps to conduct market research

Here are the steps to conduct market research:

1. **Define your research objectives:** You should start by defining your research objectives clearly. What do you want to achieve? What information do you need to make informed decisions?

2. **Determine the type of research you need:** There are two main types of market research: primary and secondary. Primary research involves gathering new data through methods like surveys, interviews, and focus groups. Secondary research involves analyzing existing data, such as reports, statistics, and industry publications.

3. **Identify your target audience:** Knowing your target audience is crucial for effective market research. Identify your ideal customer, including demographics, psychographics, and other relevant characteristics.

4. **Determine the research methodology:** There are many different research methods, including online surveys, in-person interviews, and observational research. Choose the best method for your research objectives and target audience.

5. **Collect and analyze the data:** Once you have collected your data, analyze it to identify patterns and insights. Use data visualization tools to

help you interpret the data.

6. **Draw conclusions and make recommendations:** Based on your analysis, draw conclusions about your target market and make recommendations for your business strategy.

7. **Implement your findings:** Use your research findings to improve your business strategy and make informed decisions about product development, marketing, and other aspects of your business.

Remember that market research is an ongoing process. Continually monitor your target market and adjust your strategy as needed to stay ahead of the competition.

Lets see an exmaple: Card Back

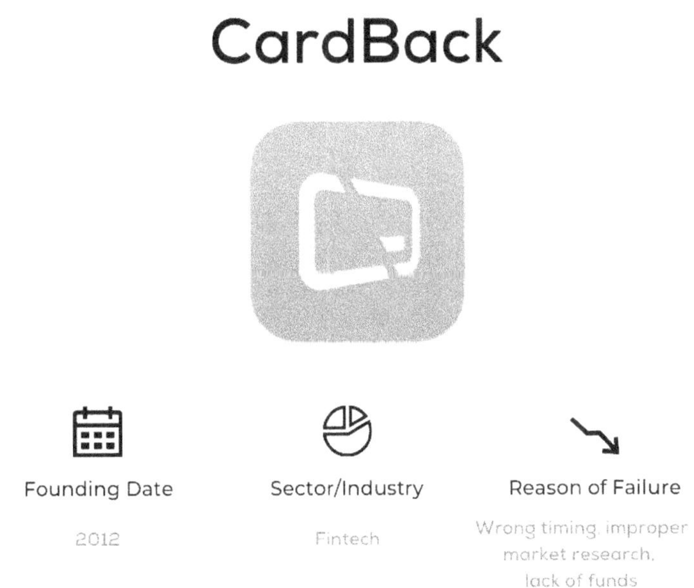

Founded by Nidhi Gurnani and Nikhil Wason, CardBack enables credit, debit, and prepaid card holders to see all offers and rewards on their cards without sharing any sensitive information.

The company had raised $170K during its five year journey. Backed by prominent angel investors such as Rajan Anandan, Sunil Kalra, and Alok Mittal, Cardback etc.

Why did Card Back failed?

The Indian market was not mature enough in 2017 as most people in the country do not have multiple credit cards.

The company needed deep pockets of investors ready to spend educating customers in safety and security of products.

They even tried to move headquarters to Singapore, a country where multiple credit card culture exists. However, the plans failed due to a large investor falling out.

Lets talk more on Primary and Secondary research

Primary Research

The data derived from the primary research is 'first-hand'. This means that you either collect the data yourself or employ someone you know to conduct research. Often, online surveys, phone interviews etc are the methods used for this. In this type of research, you have control over the entire process and can change the format in between.

Please note: The learnings from this type of research are both qualitative and quantitative.

Ways to conduct primary market research:

1. **Ethnographic research+observation:** This is in-depth research conducted in the natural setting of the object. The idea is to make the respondent totally comfortable in their habitat while the interviewer adapts themselves to their natural environment. This type of research can last from a few days to a month. Every minute detail is studied during the duration.

2. **Focus groups:** Focus group is one of the most commonly used methods for primary research. Here, a group of about 6-10 people is told about a particular release/ idea and all of them share their perceptions, thoughts and views. The best part about this is that it can be conducted remotely and is cost-effective

3. **One-to-one interview:** As the name suggests, this method involves interaction with an individual in the form of an interview. The questions

asked to the respondent here are mostly open-ended questions. This is, however, prone to bring in biased responses and the end result of this depends a lot on how the interviewer is putting the questions and their ability to facilitate responses.

4. **Surveys:** Surveys are hugely informative and helpful if conducted the best way. They can be conducted via phone, in person, on paper or via online software. It's a list of questions crafted in a way that gives you the best possible insight into how a customer feels about your product or service, your brand and the experience you provide. It can be as broad or as specific as you want.

Here is an example of primary research:

Let's say you are a market researcher working for a food company that is considering launching a new line of vegan snacks. You want to know what consumers think of the idea, so you conduct a survey to collect their opinions.

- Define the research problem: You want to know if there is a demand for vegan snacks and what consumers' attitudes are towards this type of product.

- Design the research: You design a survey that asks questions about consumers' snacking habits, their interest in vegan products, and their opinions on the proposed product.

- Collect the data: You distribute the survey to a representative sample of the target population, which may include vegans, vegetarians, and people who are interested in healthy eating.

- Analyze the data: You analyze the survey responses to identify patterns and trends in consumer attitudes towards vegan snacks.

- Interpret the results: Based on your analysis, you find that there is a significant interest in vegan snacks, particularly among health-conscious consumers. You also find that consumers are concerned about the taste and price of vegan snacks.

- Communicate the findings: You write a report summarizing your findings and recommendations for the food company, which may include suggestions for product development, pricing, and marketing strategies.

Secondary Research

Unlike the primary research methodology, secondary research uses information that is organised by sources like media houses, chambers of commerce, government agencies, private research firms etc. This information is published in different formats and shared with the general public via multiple channels like online forums, websites, newspapers, magazines, events, etc.

Ways to get secondary research results:

1. **Public sources:** Public sources such as a library is an awesome way to gather information. The best part is the information is well segregated along with the timelines. However, with the advent of the internet, the visits to the library have come down. It's always a good idea to visit one if you have enough time to find some unique publications.

2. **Commercial sources:** Local newspapers, magazines, journals, TV, radio etc. is what comes under commercial sources. Some of these might get expensive but they are one of the easiest ways to consume information.

3. **Educational institutions:** Not very commonly used, this source of collecting data can prove to be useful since a number of researchers are carried out by management and technical institutions which rarely come out.

Here's an example of secondary research:

Let's say you are a marketing analyst working for a fashion company that is considering expanding its product line to include sustainable clothing. You want to know more about the market for sustainable fashion and the attitudes of consumers towards eco-friendly clothing.

-Define the research problem: You want to know more about the sustainable fashion market and consumer attitudes towards eco-friendly clothing.

-Conduct secondary research: You search online databases and industry reports for information on sustainable fashion, such as market size, growth rates, consumer trends, and environmental regulations. You also look for academic studies and consumer surveys that provide insights into consumer attitudes towards sustainable fashion.

-Analyze the data: You analyze the data you have collected from various sources to identify patterns and trends in the sustainable fashion market and consumer attitudes towards eco-friendly clothing.

-Interpret the results: Based on your analysis, you find that the sustainable fashion market is growing rapidly and that consumers are becoming more interested in eco-friendly clothing. You also find that consumers are willing to pay a premium for sustainable clothing and that social media and influencer marketing can be effective ways to reach this audience.

-Communicate the findings: You prepare a report summarizing your findings and recommendations for the fashion company, which may include suggestions for product development, marketing strategies, and partnerships with sustainable fashion brands.

Data Analytics key to right metrics

Data analytics plays a crucial role in market research before starting a business. It helps entrepreneurs make informed decisions based on relevant and accurate data, rather than relying on guesswork or intuition. It is the process of examining and analyzing data to derive insights and make informed decisions. It involves collecting and analyzing data from various sources, including customer behavior, sales trends, and operational performance, to identify patterns and make data-driven decisions.

Data analytics is crucial for startups because it helps them to understand their target market and customers' needs, preferences, and behaviors. It enables startups to make informed decisions on pricing, product development, marketing, and customer service. With the right data, startups can identify their strengths and weaknesses and take corrective measures to improve their performance.

By leveraging data analytics, startups can also reduce their costs and increase their revenue by identifying areas for optimization and improvement. It can help them to streamline their operations, optimize their marketing strategies, and identify opportunities for new revenue streams.

Market research using data analytics can provide valuable insights into consumer behavior, market trends, competition, and other factors that can impact the success of a new business. This information can help entrepreneurs identify potential opportunities and challenges, refine their business strategy, and develop a better understanding of their target audience.

Some of the key benefits of using data analytics in market research include:

1. **Improved decision-making:** Data analytics can help entrepreneurs make more informed decisions about the feasibility and potential profitability of a new business.

2. **Better understanding of customer needs:** By analyzing customer data, businesses can gain insights into what their customers want and need, and how to best meet those needs.

3. **Competitive advantage:** Data analytics can help businesses stay ahead of the competition by identifying trends and opportunities that others may not be aware of.

4. **Cost savings:** By using data analytics to identify trends and potential risks, businesses can avoid costly mistakes and make more efficient use of their resources.

Hence, Data analytics is a critical tool for any entrepreneur looking to start a new business or grow an existing one. By leveraging data and insights, businesses can make better decisions and increase their chances of success in the market.

Types of data analytics

There are three main types of data analytics:

1. **Descriptive Analytics:** Descriptive analytics deals with summarizing past data to understand what has happened. This type of analysis is focused on describing the data and providing insights into patterns, trends, and anomalies. It can help businesses understand historical performance, identify areas for improvement, and inform decision-making.

Example: A marketing team analyzes customer data to understand which products are selling the most and which are not. Based on this analysis, they create a report that provides insights into customer behavior and helps identify areas for improvement.

2. **Predictive Analytics:** Predictive analytics involves using historical data to make predictions about future events. This type of analysis is focused on forecasting and can help businesses identify potential risks and opportunities. Predictive analytics uses machine learning and statistical models to make predictions about future outcomes.

Example: A retail store uses predictive analytics to forecast demand for a particular product during a certain time of the year. Based on historical sales data and other factors such as promotions and marketing campaigns, the store can predict how much inventory it needs to have on hand to meet customer demand.

3. **Prescriptive Analytics:** Prescriptive analytics involves using data and models to recommend actions to take in order to achieve a desired outcome.

This type of analysis is focused on optimizing decisions and can help businesses make informed choices based on data-driven insights. Prescriptive analytics uses advanced techniques such as machine learning and optimization algorithms to identify the best course of action.

Example: A healthcare provider uses prescriptive analytics to recommend the best course of treatment for a patient based on their medical history, symptoms, and other factors. The analytics model can take into account a wide range of data points to identify the most effective treatment plan, including medication dosage, lifestyle changes, and follow-up appointments.

How to conduct data analysis for your idea?

The process of conducting data analysis typically involves the following steps:

1. **Define the Problem:** Start by defining the problem you want to solve or the question you want to answer with your analysis. This will help you identify the data you need to collect and the analysis techniques you should use.

Example: You want to understand why your website is not generating as many leads as you had hoped.

2. **Collect the Data**: Gather the data you need to conduct your analysis. This may involve collecting data from different sources such as website analytics, customer surveys, or sales reports.

Example: You collect data on website traffic, conversion rates, bounce rates, and lead generation efforts.

3. **Clean and Prepare the Data:** Once you have collected the data, you will need to clean and prepare it for analysis. This may involve removing duplicates, fixing errors, and formatting the data in a way that makes it easy to analyze.

Example: You remove any incomplete or duplicate data, fix any formatting issues, and ensure that all the data is in a consistent format.

4. **Conduct the Analysis:** Use the appropriate data analysis techniques to answer your research question or solve your problem. This may involve creating charts and graphs, performing statistical analysis, or using machine learning algorithms.

Example: You use regression analysis to identify which website metrics are most closely correlated with lead generation.

5. **Interpret the Results:** Once you have completed your analysis, you will need to interpret the results and draw conclusions. This may involve identifying patterns, trends, and anomalies in the data.

Example: You find that website traffic and time spent on the website are the two most important factors in generating leads.

6. **Communicate the Findings:** Finally, you will need to communicate your findings to others. This may involve creating a report, presentation, or dashboard to share with stakeholders.

Example: You create a report that summarizes your findings and recommends specific changes to the website to improve lead generation.

Overall, the process of conducting data analysis requires a combination of technical skills, domain knowledge, and critical thinking. It is essential to use the right tools and techniques to ensure that the data analysis is accurate, reliable, and provides valuable insights for decision-making.

Tools that can help in data analytics

There are many tools available that can help with data analytics. Here are some examples:

-**Microsoft Excel**: Excel is a widely used spreadsheet program that can be used for data analysis. It includes various features such as sorting, filtering, and pivot tables that make it easy to organize and analyze data.

-**Tableau**: Tableau is a powerful data visualization tool that allows users to create interactive charts and graphs from their data. It can be used to identify patterns and trends in large datasets and communicate insights effectively.

-**Python**: Python is a programming language that is popular in data analytics and machine learning. It has many libraries and frameworks available for data manipulation and analysis, including Pandas and NumPy.

-**Google Analytics**: Google Analytics is a web analytics tool that can be used to track website traffic and user behavior. It provides insights into how visitors interact with a website, including which pages they visit, how long they stay, and where they come from.

-**R**: R is a programming language and environment for statistical computing and graphics. It includes a wide range of libraries and packages for data manipulation, analysis, and visualization.

-**IBM SPSS**: IBM SPSS is a software suite that can be used for data analysis and statistical modeling. It includes features for data cleaning, descriptive statistics, and predictive analytics.

-**SAS**: SAS is a software suite for data management, analysis, and visualization. It includes a wide range of tools and features for data integration, data mining, and statistical modeling.

These are just a few examples of the many tools available for data analytics. The choice of tool will depend on the specific needs of the business or project, as well as the expertise of the user.

Find a Problem

Finding a problem or choosing the right market opportunity is the first step in starting a successful startup. Moreover, Validating your business idea before starting up is crucial to increase the likelihood of success and reduce the risk of failure.

How to find a problem or a market opportunity?

"If I were given one hour to save the planet, I would spend 59 minutes defining the problem and one minute resolving it," Albert Einstein said.

There's never been a better time to start a new business. Sometimes you simply need an idea that inspires you. The right idea can help you find a purpose. And the purpose is where it all starts — the WHY.

As an entrepreneur, how confident are you that you fully understand your customer's pain points or their job to be done? Entrepreneurs I first meet tend to start selling me on their solution before explaining the problem they are trying to solve. There is little evidence that they've done true discovery work to validate the problem or their target customers.

It is quite remarkable that a 17-year-old boy could come up with a hotel aggregator platform that has since become more successful than running a single hotel chain. This is precisely what has happened with OYO, a brand that has rapidly grown in popularity and success.

The Problem-Definition Process

The problem definition process involves identifying, clarifying, and describing a problem or issue that needs to be addressed. The following are the typical steps involved in the problem definition process:

1. **Identify the problem:** The first step is to identify the problem that needs to be solved. This could involve gathering information from various sources, such as customer feedback, employee input, or market research.

2. **Define the problem**: Once the problem has been identified, it is important to clearly define it. This involves stating the problem in clear and concise terms, and ensuring that everyone involved understands the problem in the same way.

3. **Gather data**: After defining the problem, it is important to gather relevant data to support the problem statement. This could involve collecting data from internal or external sources, such as customer surveys, financial reports, or industry research.

4. **Analyze the data**: Once the data has been collected, it is important to analyze it to gain insights into the problem. This could involve using statistical methods, trend analysis, or other techniques to identify patterns and trends in the data.

5. **Identify possible solutions**: Based on the analysis of the data, it is important to identify possible solutions to the problem. This could involve brainstorming sessions, research, or consulting with experts in the field.

7. **Evaluate the solutions**: After identifying possible solutions, it is important to evaluate them to determine which ones are the most viable. This could involve weighing the pros and cons of each solution, considering the costs and benefits, and assessing the feasibility of each option.

8. **Select the best solution**: Finally, based on the evaluation of the solutions, it is important to select the best solution and develop a plan to implement it. This could involve outlining the steps required to implement the solution, assigning responsibilities to team members, and setting timelines and deadlines.

6 Step process to identify a right problem

Here are some steps you can follow to help you identify a problem or market opportunity:

1. **Identify your interests and skills:** Start by considering what you are passionate about or what skills you have. This will help you identify potential areas of focus for your startup.

2. **Research the market:** Look at what is currently available in the market and identify areas where there may be a gap or an unmet need.

3. **Talk to potential customers:** Engage with potential customers to understand their pain points, needs, and challenges. This will help you identify potential areas where you can provide value.

4. **Analyse the competition:** Analyse the competition and identify areas where they may be lacking or where you can provide a unique value proposition.

5. **Conduct a SWOT analysis:** Conduct a SWOT (Strengths, Weaknesses, Opportunities, Threats) analysis of your potential market opportunity to help you identify potential challenges and opportunities.

6. **Consider the scalability and feasibility:** Finally, consider the scalability and feasibility of your idea. Is it something that can grow and sustain over time? Is it something that you have the resources and capabilities to execute?

By following these steps, you can help narrow down your options and identify a problem or market opportunity that is a good fit for your skills and interests, has a potential customer base, and is scalable and feasible.

Is it the right problem to solve?

I am sure by now you must have shortlisted the problem that you are willing to solve and begin your entrepreneurship journey with.

Stop now if you have started building the solution without validating the problem you will be solving.

As an entrepreneur, you need to ensure that the problem you are solving is the right problem, hence it needs an another level of validation before you start working on it.

- **Conduct Research**

Conduct thorough research to understand the problem you are trying to solve. Analyze the market trends, customer needs, and pain points to validate the problem's existence.

-**Talk to your target audience**

Engage with your potential customers to understand their pain points and how they currently address the problem. This feedback will help you to refine your solution and ensure that it aligns with their needs.You need to ensure that the problem you are solving is the right problem to be solved in order to create a solution that will address your target audience's needs effectively.

Ritesh Agarwal stayed stayed at over 100 bed-and-breakfast rooms while running Oravel, soon discovered that the problem for these portals was not discovery. "The big problem was that these portals are not standardised. Hence, OYO was founded to solve the problem. What can be a better example of problem validation than this?

Let's do it together!

Step 1: Establish the Need for a Solution

The purpose of this step is to articulate the problem in the simplest terms possible: "We are looking for X in order to achieve Z as measured by W." Such a statement, akin to an elevator pitch, is a call to arms that clarifies the importance of the issue and helps secure resources to address it. This initial framing answers three questions:

- **What is the basic need?**

This is the essential problem, stated clearly and concisely. It is important at this stage to focus on the need that's at the heart of the problem instead of jumping to a solution. Defining the scope is also important.

- **What is the desired outcome?**

Answering this question requires understanding the perspectives of customers and other beneficiaries. Again, avoid the temptation to favour a particular solution or approach. This question should be addressed qualitatively and quantitatively whenever possible.

- **Who stands to benefit and why?**

Answering this question compels you to identify all potential customers and beneficiaries. If the problem you want to solve is industrywide, it's crucial to understand why the market has failed to address it.

Step 2: Justify the Need

The purpose of answering the questions in this step is to explain why you should attempt to solve the problem.

- **Is the effort aligned with our strategy?**

In other words, will satisfying the need serve your strategic goals? It is not unusual for you to be working on problems that are no longer in sync with its strategy or mission.

- **What are the desired benefits for you, and how will we measure them?**

In for-profit companies, the desired benefit could be to reach a revenue target, attain a certain market share, or achieve specific cycle-time improvements.

Step 3: Contextualize the Problem

Examining past efforts to find a solution can save time and resources and generate highly innovative thinking. If the problem is industrywide, it's crucial to understand why the market has failed to address it.

Step 4: Write the Problem Statement

Now it's time to write a full description of the problem you're seeking to solve and the requirements the solution must meet. The problem statement, which captures all that you have learned through answering the questions in the previous steps, helps establish a consensus on what a viable solution would be and what resources would be required to achieve it.

Surveys, one of the best tool to validate

Surveys can be an effective tool for problem validation. Surveys allow you to gather data from a large number of people quickly and efficiently, providing you with insights into the opinions, behaviours, and experiences of your target audience.

When conducting a survey for problem validation, you can use it to:

1. **Identify pain points:** Surveys can help you identify the specific problems that your target audience is facing, providing you with valuable information on what needs to be addressed.

2. **Validate assumptions:** Surveys can help you test assumptions about your target audience and the problems they face. By asking targeted questions, you can validate whether or not your assumptions are accurate.

3. **Gather feedback:** Surveys can help you gather feedback on potential solutions to the problems you've identified. By presenting different solutions to your target audience and asking for their opinions, you can gain valuable insights into what approaches are likely to be successful.

4. **Prioritise features:** Surveys can also help you prioritise the features or solutions that your target audience values the most. By asking questions about which features are most important to them, you can focus your efforts on building solutions that are more likely to be adopted.

Surveys can be an important tool for problem validation, allowing you to gather valuable insights from your target audience quickly and efficiently. However, it's important to design your survey carefully, ensuring that you're asking the right questions and targeting the right audience.

Here are some steps to consider when designing surveys:

- **Determine the goal of the survey:** The first step is to identify the purpose of the survey. What is the problem you are trying to solve? What information are you looking to gather?

- **Define the target audience:** Who are you trying to survey? Determine the characteristics of the audience you want to reach (e.g., age, gender, occupation, etc.).

- **Choose the right survey method:** There are different methods to conduct surveys, such as online surveys, telephone surveys, mail surveys, and in-person surveys. Choose the method that works best for your target audience.

- **Develop the survey questions:** Develop questions that will elicit the information you need. Use clear and concise language and avoid leading questions. You can also use open-ended questions to encourage respondents to provide detailed answers.

- **Test the survey:** Before launching the survey, test it with a small group of people to ensure the questions are clear and easy to understand.

- **Launch the survey:** Once you have finalized the survey questions, launch the survey using your chosen method.

- **Analyze the results:** Analyze the data collected from the survey and use it to validate your problem and identify any areas that need improvement.

When designing questions for the survey, consider asking questions that will provide insights into the following areas:

-**The respondent's understanding of the problem you are trying to solve**

-The frequency and severity of the problem

-The respondent's current behavior related to the problem

-The respondent's willingness to try a new solution

-The potential benefits and drawbacks of a new solution

By considering these factors and designing appropriate questions, you can create a survey that provides valuable insights into the problem you are trying to solve.

"When I started my entrepreneurial journey, I ensured to speak to more than 100 people who could be my potential target audience to ensure if I am on the right direction to finalise the problem I want to solve.

What do Urban Company, Paytm, Delhivery, Cred, Ola, etc. have in common – they're Indian start-ups. They are success stories that inspire entrepreneurs to hold on to their vision. The main reason these ventures succeeded in light of the many challenges faced by start-ups in India is that they attacked a real need.

A good idea solves a problem and/or fulfills a certain need people have. It should be both something those people are willing to pay for and something that can be scaled."

CHAPTER FOUR

Define your Target audience

The target audience for a startup is the specific group of people or businesses that the company aims to reach and serve with its products or services. This group of people or businesses should have a need or desire for the startup's offerings and be willing to pay for them. Identifying a target audience is essential for a startup to create a successful marketing strategy and allocate resources effectively.

How to define target audience?

Defining a target audience involves identifying the specific group of people who are most likely to be interested in your product, service, or message. Here are some steps you can follow to define your target audience:

1. **Conduct market research:** This involves gathering data about your target audience, including their demographics (age, gender, income, etc.), psychographics (values, interests, personality, etc.), behaviors, and attitudes towards your product or service.

2. **Use social media analytics:** Social media platforms provide valuable data on your target audience, such as their engagement with your content, demographics, and interests. Analyzing this data can help you tailor your messaging to better resonate with your target audience.

3. **Develop buyer personas:** A buyer persona is a fictional representation of your ideal customer, based on real data and market research. It includes information such as their age, job title, income, values, interests, and pain points.

4. **Conduct surveys and focus groups:** Surveys and focus groups can help you gather direct feedback from your target audience about their opinions, behaviors, and needs. This can help you identify areas for improvement in your product or service and tailor your messaging

accordingly.

5. **Monitor industry trends:** Staying up-to-date on industry trends can help you anticipate changes in your target audience's behavior and adjust your marketing strategies accordingly.

By analyzing your target audience through these various methods, you can gain a better understanding of who they are, what they need, and how to effectively communicate with them.

Types of target audience

There are several types of target audiences, including:

Target audience refers to a specific group of people that a product, service, or message is intended for. Here are some types of target audiences with examples:

1. **Demographic target audience:** This type of target audience is defined by specific demographic factors such as age, gender, income, education level, and marital status. For example, a company that sells luxury cars may target high-income individuals who are married, aged 35-50, and have a postgraduate degree.

2. **Geographic target audience:** This type of target audience is defined by specific geographic locations such as countries, cities, or neighborhoods. For example, a local restaurant may target people who live or work within a specific zip code.

3. **Psychographic target audience:** This type of target audience is defined by personality traits, values, attitudes, interests, and lifestyles. For example, a company that sells outdoor gear may target people who are adventurous, environmentally conscious, and enjoy outdoor activities.

4. **Behavioral target audience:** This type of target audience is defined by specific behaviors such as buying habits, product usage, and response to marketing messages. For example, an online retailer may target people who frequently buy organic and natural products.

5. **Firmographic target audience:** This type of target audience is defined by specific characteristics of the organizations or businesses that are being targeted. For example, a B2B software company may target small and medium-sized businesses in a specific industry or geographic location.

6. **Generational target audience:** This type of target audience is defined by specific generational cohorts such as Baby Boomers, Gen X, Millennials, and Gen Z. For example, a clothing brand may target Millennials who are

known for valuing authenticity and sustainability.

These are just a few examples of target audiences, and it's important to note that a single product or service may have multiple target audiences based on different factors.

- Let's say the startup is a company that sells organic baby food online. To define its target audience, the startup might consider:

- Demographic characteristics: The startup's target audience could be parents or caregivers of infants and toddlers, typically between the ages of 25-45 years old, who are health-conscious and value organic food for their children.

- Psychographic characteristics: The target audience may be environmentally conscious, value health and wellness, and prioritize their child's nutrition and development.

- Geographic location: The target audience may live in urban or suburban areas where access to organic food and grocery stores is limited or inconvenient.

- Behavior: The target audience may actively seek out and purchase organic food products for their families, and are willing to pay a premium price for high-quality, convenient, and trustworthy products.

Based on this analysis, the startup can tailor its marketing messages and product offerings to appeal to its target audience. For example, the company could emphasize the health benefits of organic baby food, showcase its convenient online ordering and delivery process, and use eco-friendly packaging materials to appeal to environmentally conscious parents. By focusing on the specific needs and preferences of its target audience, the startup can increase the likelihood of success and grow its customer base over time.

Create Impact in target audience

Creating an impact in your target audience requires a thoughtful and intentional approach. Here are some tips on how to do so:

1. **Understand your target audience**: The first step to creating an impact in your target audience is to understand who they are, what they care about, and what motivates them. Conduct market research, analyze your customer data, and gather insights from social media to gain a deeper understanding of your audience.

2. **Develop a clear message**: Once you understand your audience, develop a clear message that resonates with them. Your message should be concise, memorable, and aligned with your brand's values and mission.

3. **Use emotional appeal**: Emotions are a powerful tool for creating impact in your target audience. Use emotional appeal to connect with your audience on a deeper level and inspire them to take action.

4. **Use storytelling**: Storytelling is an effective way to create impact in your target audience. Use storytelling to illustrate your message in a compelling and relatable way.

5. **Choose the right channels**: Choose the right channels to reach your target audience. Use a mix of channels, such as social media, email marketing, and advertising, to ensure your message reaches your target audience where they are most active.

6. **Measure impact**: Measure the impact of your message to see how it resonated with your target audience. Use metrics such as engagement rates, website traffic, and sales to track the effectiveness of your message and make adjustments as needed.

Overall, creating an impact in your target audience requires a deep understanding of your audience, a clear message, emotional appeal, storytelling, the right channels, and measurement. By following these tips, you can create an impact that resonates with your target audience and drives business results.

Creating impact in your target audience requires careful planning and execution. Here's an example of how to create impact in your target audience:

- Let's say you are a non-profit organization focused on environmental conservation. Your target audience is young adults who are environmentally conscious and are interested in making a positive impact on the environment.

- To create impact in this target audience, you could organize an event focused on sustainability and conservation. This event could include talks by experts in the field, interactive exhibits showcasing sustainable practices, and workshops on how to live a more sustainable lifestyle.

- You could also collaborate with local businesses and organizations to provide eco-friendly products and services at the event, such as reusable water bottles, compostable utensils, and organic food options.

- To further increase the impact of the event, you could use social media to promote it and encourage attendees to share their experiences on their own social media accounts. You could also provide resources and follow-up information after the event to help attendees continue to make positive changes in their own lives.

By carefully planning and executing this event, you would create a meaningful impact in your target audience by educating them on sustainable practices and inspiring them to take action in their own lives.

Feedback Mechanism

Feedback mechanisms are essential in understanding your target audience's needs, preferences, and opinions. Here are some feedback mechanisms you can use to gather insights from your target audience:

1. **Surveys:** Surveys are a great way to gather quantitative data on your target audience's preferences, opinions, and behaviors. You can distribute surveys through various channels such as email, social media, and website pop-ups.

2. **Focus Groups:** Focus groups are a qualitative research method where you gather a small group of individuals from your target audience to discuss their experiences, opinions, and attitudes towards your product or service. Focus groups can provide valuable insights into your target audience's needs and expectations.

3. **User Testing:** User testing involves observing your target audience as they use your product or service and providing feedback on their experience. User testing can help you identify usability issues and areas for improvement.

4. **Online Reviews:** Online reviews can provide valuable feedback from your target audience. You can monitor and respond to online reviews to gain insights into what your target audience likes and dislikes about your product or service.

5. **Social Media Listening**: Social media listening involves monitoring social media platforms for mentions of your brand or product. You can use

social media listening tools to track and analyze these mentions, gaining insights into your target audience's opinions and preferences.

By incorporating these feedback mechanisms into your marketing strategy, you can gain a better understanding of your target audience's needs and preferences, allowing you to tailor your messaging and offerings to better meet their expectations.

Customer Behaviour

Understanding customer behavior is critical before building a solution for several reasons:

- **Identifying customer needs:** Understanding customer behavior helps you identify the needs and pain points of your target audience. By understanding their behavior, you can determine what they are looking for, what they value, and what problems they need to solve.

- **Tailoring the solution**: Once you understand the needs and pain points of your target audience, you can tailor your solution to meet their specific needs. This increases the chances of your solution being adopted and achieving success in the market.

- **Improving the user experience:** Understanding customer behavior can help you design a user experience that is intuitive, efficient, and effective. By designing a solution that is easy to use and aligns with the way customers think and behave, you can increase the chances of user adoption and satisfaction.

- **Addressing customer objections:** By understanding customer behavior, you can anticipate objections and barriers that may prevent them from adopting your solution. This allows you to proactively address these objections and create a solution that overcomes these barriers.

- **Differentiating from competitors:** Understanding customer behavior can also help you differentiate your solution from competitors. By designing a solution that is tailored to the needs and behaviors of your target audience, you can create a unique value proposition that sets you apart from the competition.

Overall, understanding customer behavior is critical for building a successful solution. By taking the time to understand your target audience, you can design a solution that meets their needs, improves the user experience, and sets you apart from the competition.

CHAPTER FIVE

How to build a sellable solution?

If a solution solves a problem, value is generated. As a startup, that's what you want. In the end, all successful innovations are appropriate combinations of problems and solutions. Within the startup journey, problem-solution fit is an important milestone. Problem-solution fit is often assumed, yet not always checked thoroughly.

What Is Problem-Solution Fit?

Problem-solution fit is a concept in entrepreneurship and startup development that refers to the degree of alignment between a specific problem and the solution provided by a product or service. In other words, it is the extent to which a product or service satisfies a real and pressing need in the market.

To achieve problem-solution fit, entrepreneurs and startups need to identify a real problem that potential customers are experiencing, and then develop a solution that effectively addresses that problem. As we discussed in the last chapter this requires a deep understanding of the market, the target customers, and their pain points, as well as an ability to develop and iterate on solutions that meet those needs.

When a product or service achieves problem-solution fit, it is more likely to be successful because it has a clear value proposition that resonates with customers. This can lead to increased customer adoption, retention, and revenue growth, and can also help establish a strong brand reputation and a loyal customer base.

The problem-solution fit is when you-

1. **Validate that the problem exists:** When you validate your problem hypothesis using real-world data and feedback. That is, you gather information from real users to determine whether or not they care about the pain point you're trying to solve.

2. **Validate that your solution solves the problem:** When you validate that the target audience appreciates the value your solution delivers to them.

The problem-solution fit precedes the product development and forms the foundation upon which a company is built. It helps you answer the basics startup-related questions before you even start your startup.

- *Do people actually have the problem that you think they have?*
- *How do they solve the problem now?*
- *Does your proposed solution make a meaningful difference?*

Once you're satisfied with the answers, you use this solution to develop a saleable product and start acquiring customers.

Why Achieving A Problem Solution Fit Important?

Achieving problem-solution fit is essential to the success of any new business. Because without it, you're essentially just guessing that your idea is going to work. And if you want to be successful, you need more than just a guess. Achieving problem-solution fit is critical for the success of a startup or new product/service offering for several reasons:

1. **Validates the idea:** By achieving problem-solution fit, the startup or entrepreneur is validating the idea that there is a real need or pain point in the market that their product/service is addressing. This provides confidence that there is demand for the offering and can help attract investors, customers, and talent.

2. **Drives customer adoption:** If a product/service provides a solution to a real problem that customers are experiencing, it is more likely to be adopted and used. This can drive customer acquisition and retention, resulting in revenue growth.

3. **Creates a competitive advantage:** Achieving problem-solution fit can help differentiate the product/service from competitors and create a

sustainable competitive advantage. This is because a product/service that effectively addresses a real problem is more likely to be preferred by customers over competing offerings.

4. **Enables further product development:** Once problem-solution fit is achieved, entrepreneurs can focus on further developing and refining the product/service to enhance its value proposition and meet evolving customer needs. This can lead to continued growth and success.

Overall, achieving problem-solution fit is a critical step in the early stages of a startup or new product/service offering, and is essential for building a successful and sustainable business.

When Should You Look For A Problem-Solution Fit?

If you're an entrepreneur or someone who is working on a new project or idea, it's important to look for a problem-solution fit as early as possible. This means that you need to identify a real problem that people are experiencing, and then come up with a solution that solves that problem.

Looking for a problem-solution fit early on can help you save time and resources by ensuring that you're building something that people actually want and need. It can also help you avoid investing in a solution that doesn't have a market or that doesn't solve a real problem.

Here are some specific situations when you should look for a problem-solution fit:

- **When you're starting a new business or project.**
- **When you're considering launching a new product or service.**
- **When you're pivoting your existing business or product in a new direction.**
- **When you're experiencing a lack of traction or growth with your current business or product.**
- **When you're considering investing in a new market or industry.**

In all of these situations, it's important to conduct research and talk to potential customers to identify the real problems they're facing and to understand whether your solution can solve those problems. By doing this early on, you can increase your chances of success and avoid wasting time and resources on solutions that don't work.

How To Achieve Problem-Solution Fit

The key to achieving a problem-solution fit lies in identifying the right people to talk to, gathering data from them, and then analysing the results. This is easier said than done, of course. But this can be done by following two simple steps –

- Develop A Customer Profile

The customer profile section helps you to understand your target audience in greater detail. This process will give you answers to the most important customer-related questions that will take you closer to your offering –

- *Who are they? (Persona)*
- *What jobs do they need to get done? (Jobs-to-be-done)*
- *What problems do they face while doing the job? (Pain points)*
- *What do they gain by completing the job? (Desired Outcomes)*

-The Customer Persona

The customer persona is a semi-fictional representation of your ideal customer based on market research and real data about your existing customers. Creating a customer persona helps you understand your target audience better. It includes information like –

- Demographics: Age, gender, location, education, job title
- Psychographics: Lifestyle, values, interests, attitudes
- Behavioural patterns: Buying habits, online behaviour, communication preferences

- The Job-To-Be-Done

Consider your customer's job-to-be-done as the reason why they need your solution.

For example, imagine that your target customer is a busy professional who wants to increase their productivity. This "job" might include managing their email, calendars and social media accounts all in one place.

-Painpoints

What are the challenges and frustrations your target customers experience while completing the job?

For example, busy professionals might find it difficult to keep track of their different accounts and feel constantly bombarded with notifications.

-Desired outcomes

What are the desired results or outcomes your customer hopes to achieve by completing the job?

For example, they want to be able to quickly find the information they need and minimise interruptions.

-Conduct Customer Interviews

The customer profile results in a hypothesis about the problem your target customers face.

You need to talk to actual people who match your persona to validate this hypothesis. This is done by conducting customer interviews, and its goal is to collect qualitative and quantitative data that will help you better understand your users' needs. Problem interviews are typically exploratory in nature. These are unstructured interviews in which you ask open-ended questions to better understand the problem.

Take this scenario, for example –

You're building a productivity app for busy professionals.

Your previous hypotheses suggested that the primary challenge your customers face is managing their email, calendars and social media accounts all in one place.

To verify this hypothesis, you conduct exploratory interviews with a small group of users where you ask questions like – "Tell me about the biggest challenges you face at work", and "How do you currently manage your email, calendar and social media accounts?".

From the responses, you narrow down on the pain points and start to form a clearer picture of the problem.

This feedback helps you validate (or invalidate) your previous assumptions and makes it easier to develop a solution that meets the needs of your target customers.

- Develop A Solutions Profile

The solutions profile describes the solution you plan to offer that addresses your customers' desired outcomes. It results from your customer interviews and should be based on actual feedback, not assumptions. You develop a solutions profile by answering:

- How do you help the customer get their job done?
- How do you address and solve their pain points?

- What are the desired outcomes for the customer?

A solutions profile might look something like this:

Our productivity app helps busy professionals manage their email, calendar and social media accounts all in one place. It offers a unified inbox that shows all your messages from different accounts in one place and allows you to switch between them with just a few taps quickly. Additionally, it includes a centralised calendar that lets you schedule meetings and appointments without having to switch between multiple apps. And finally, we provide tools for managing your social media accounts so you never miss an important update again!

- Conduct Confirmation Interviews

Your solution profile is based on your customer interviews, but it's important to validate your problem-solution fit with actual users before you start building anything. This is done using confirmation interviews. Confirmation interviews are structured with a focus on testing the proposed solution. In these interviews, you focus on verifying the findings of your exploratory interviews along with the proposed solution. This is done by asking more specific but open-ended questions like – *"How would you feel if you had a unified inbox for all your email accounts?", "What would be the biggest benefit of having a centralised calendar?"*.

The goal of confirmation interviews is not to get detailed feedback on the proposed solution, but to validate that the solution solves the problem in a way that is valuable to the customer.

Problem-Solution Fit Example

Here is an example of how a startup can achieve problem-solution fit:

Let's say that a startup is looking to solve the problem of food waste in households. The first step would be to conduct research to understand the scope of the problem, the reasons why households waste food, and the potential impact of food waste on the environment.

After identifying the problem, the startup needs to define its target market. In this case, the target market could be households that are conscious about their impact on the environment and are looking for ways to reduce their food waste.

The startup could then develop a solution, such as a mobile app that helps households track their food inventory, plan their meals, and reduce their waste by suggesting recipes that use up ingredients that are about to expire.

To test the solution, the startup could conduct user surveys and focus groups to gather feedback on the app's usability, effectiveness, and overall value. Based on this feedback, the startup may need to iterate and refine the solution until it achieves problem-solution fit.

Once the startup has achieved problem-solution fit, it can launch the app and monitor its performance by tracking key metrics, such as user engagement, retention, and customer satisfaction. The startup can also continue to iterate and refine the app based on ongoing feedback and data analysis to ensure that it remains aligned with the needs of its target market.

In this example, the startup achieved problem-solution fit by identifying a specific problem, defining its target market, developing a solution that addresses the problem in a unique and effective way, and continuously iterating and refining the solution based on feedback and data analysis.

Types of solutions to startup

There are several types of solutions that a startup can offer, depending on the industry and market they are targeting. Here are some examples of different types of startup solutions:

1. **Product-based solutions:** These startups create and sell physical products to consumers or other businesses. Examples include Tesla, Casper, and Peloton.

2. **Service-based solutions:** These startups offer services to customers, such as consulting, marketing, or software development. Examples include Deloitte, HubSpot, and Wix.

3. **Marketplace solutions:** These startups act as intermediaries between buyers and sellers, facilitating transactions and taking a commission or fee. Examples include Airbnb, Uber, and Etsy.

4. **Subscription-based solutions:** These startups charge customers a recurring fee for access to a product or service. Examples include Netflix, Spotify, and Amazon Prime.

5. **Platform solutions:** These startups create a platform that allows other businesses or individuals to build upon or use their technology. Examples include Amazon Web Services, Microsoft Azure, and Google Cloud Platform.

6. **Social Impact solutions:** These startups focus on solving social or environmental problems through their products or services. Examples include TOMS, Warby Parker, and Patagonia.

7. **Hybrid solutions:** Some startups may combine multiple types of solutions, such as a product-based startup that also offers a subscription service. Examples include Dollar Shave Club and HelloFresh.

The type of solution a startup chooses to offer will depend on their specific goals and the needs of their target market. It's important for startups to carefully research and validate their ideas before developing a solution to ensure they are providing a valuable and viable solution to their customers.

CHAPTER SIX

Build a prototype

What is a prototype?

A prototype is an early sample, model, or release of a product or idea that is used to test or evaluate the concept and determine if it's feasible, functional, and meets the intended requirements. It is usually a preliminary version that may lack some features, be incomplete or have errors, but serves as a basis for future iterations and improvements.

Prototypes can be physical or digital, and they are commonly used in fields such as engineering, design, software development, and manufacturing to validate assumptions, gather feedback, and make informed decisions.

What Is Prototyping?

Prototyping is the process of creating a preliminary version or model of a product, service, or idea to test its feasibility, functionality, and design. It is an iterative and interactive approach that involves building, testing, and refining prototypes until a satisfactory solution is achieved.

The purpose of prototyping is to validate assumptions, generate feedback from stakeholders and end-users, identify potential issues, and refine the concept to improve its performance, usability, and user experience. Prototyping can take various forms, such as sketches, wireframes, mockups, 3D models, functional prototypes, and minimum viable products (MVPs), depending on the project's needs and goals.

Prototyping is widely used in fields such as product development, software engineering, user experience design, and innovation, where the ability to quickly and iteratively test and refine ideas can lead to better products and solutions.

Steps of Prototyping

The steps of prototyping can vary depending on the project's scope and goals, but here are some general steps that are commonly followed in the prototyping process:

1. **Identify the problem**: Define the problem you are trying to solve and understand the user's needs and requirements. This step is critical to ensure that the prototype addresses the right problem.

2. **Develop ideas:** Brainstorm potential solutions and generate ideas to solve the problem. Encourage creativity and involve stakeholders and end-users in the ideation process.

3. **Create a design:** Use the ideas generated to create a preliminary design. This can be in the form of sketches, wireframes, or mockups.

4. **Build a prototype:** Use the design to build a working prototype. Depending on the project's needs, this could be a low-fidelity or high-fidelity prototype.

5.**Test the prototype**: Conduct testing with end-users to gather feedback and identify areas for improvement. This can be done through user testing or usability testing.

6. **Refine the prototype:** Use the feedback received to refine the prototype and make improvements. This could involve making changes to the design or functionality.

7, **Repeat:** Repeat the prototyping process, incorporating the changes and feedback received from testing, until a satisfactory solution is achieved.

Overall, the prototyping process is iterative and involves constant feedback and refinement to create a successful final product.

Types of prototypes

There are various types of prototypes that can be created depending on the project's needs and goals. Here are some common types of prototypes:

1. **Low-Fidelity Prototypes:** These are early-stage prototypes that use simple materials such as paper, cardboard, or wireframes to represent the concept's basic functionality and design. Low-fidelity prototypes are quick and easy to create, making them ideal for initial testing and feedback.

2. **High-Fidelity Prototypes:** These prototypes use more advanced materials and technologies to create a realistic representation of the final product. High-fidelity prototypes can include functional prototypes or 3D-printed models that simulate the final product's form and function.

3. **Interactive Prototypes:** These prototypes use software or hardware to create an interactive experience for the user. They can include interactive wireframes, clickable mockups, or functional prototypes that allow users to interact with the product.

4. **Virtual Prototypes:** These prototypes use computer-aided design (CAD) software to create a 3D model of the product. Virtual prototypes can be used to test the product's design and functionality, as well as simulate its performance under various conditions.

5. **Minimum Viable Product (MVP):** An MVP is a functional prototype that includes only the essential features required to test the product's viability and value proposition. An MVP is typically used in software development and startup environments to validate assumptions and gather feedback from early adopters.

Overall, the type of prototype chosen depends on the project's goals, the level of fidelity required, and the resources available for development and testing.

What Are the Benefits of Prototyping?

Prototyping offers numerous benefits in product design and development, including:

- **Refining the Concept:** Prototyping allows designers and developers to test their ideas and refine them before investing significant resources into the final product. This can help identify potential problems and make necessary adjustments.

- **Saving Time and Money:** By identifying design issues early on, prototyping can save time and money in the long run. It's much easier to make changes to a prototype than to modify a finished product.

- **Improving Communication:** Prototypes can be used to communicate ideas and designs to stakeholders and potential customers. This can help ensure everyone involved is on the same page and can help generate valuable feedback.

- **Reducing Risk:** Prototyping can help identify potential risks and mitigate them before they become major issues. This can help reduce the risk of failure or costly mistakes down the road.

- **Enhancing Innovation:** Prototyping encourages experimentation and creativity, which can lead to innovative ideas and solutions.

Prototyping is a valuable tool in the design and development process that can help save time and money, reduce risk, and enhance innovation.

What Are the Stages of Prototyping?

Prototype product development is the process of taking a product from initial conception to marketable form. It includes market research, product design, prototyping, testing, production, and packaging. prototype product development is a key part of bringing a new product to market and is often one of the most difficult and expensive stages of the process.

There are a number of factors to consider during the prototype development process, such as function, form, manufacturability, and cost.

Stages of prototype development:

- **Conceptualisation:** This is the initial stage where ideas and concepts are brainstormed, and sketches or mockups are created to illustrate the basic concept.

- **Low-Fidelity Prototyping:** In this stage, rough models or basic mockups are created using low-cost materials like cardboard, paper, or clay. These prototypes are used to test and refine the concept and identify potential design issues.

- **High-Fidelity Prototyping:** This stage involves creating more detailed and accurate prototypes using more advanced materials like 3D printers, CNC machines, or injection molding. These prototypes are closer to the final product and are used to test functionality, user experience, and aesthetics.

- **Testing and Evaluation:** In this stage, the prototype is tested and evaluated to ensure it meets the desired specifications and requirements. User feedback is also collected to identify areas for improvement.

- **Refinement and Iteration:** Based on the feedback received during testing and evaluation, the prototype is refined and improved through multiple iterations until the final product is achieved.

- **Production:** Once the final prototype is approved, it can be sent to production for mass manufacturing.

These stages of prototyping can be repeated multiple times throughout the design and development process until the desired outcome is achieved.

What Are Data-Driven Prototyping Tools?

Some of the Prototyping Tools That You Can Use To Build Successful Prototypes Are:

- Invision
- Webflow
- Axure
- Sketch
- Adobe XD
- Justinmind

Lets build a prototype!

Building a basic prototype for a brand and website involves several steps. Below are the steps with examples:

Step1: Determine your brand name

Choosing the right name for your startup is an important step in building your brand identity. A strong brand name can help differentiate your company from competitors, build trust with customers, and establish a lasting impression in the marketplace. Here are some steps to consider when determining a brand name for your startup:

1. **Determine your brand identity:** Before choosing a name, you should have a clear idea of your brand's values, mission, and target audience. Your brand name should reflect these values and appeal to your target market.

2. **Brainstorm potential names:** Once you have a clear idea of your brand identity, start brainstorming potential names. Consider using a name that is memorable, easy to pronounce, and easy to spell. You can also use descriptive words or a play on words to create a unique and catchy name.

3. **Check availability**: Once you have a list of potential names, check to see if they are available as a domain name and social media handles. This will help ensure that you can use the name for your website and social

media accounts.

4. **Conduct a trademark search**: Before finalizing your brand name, conduct a trademark search to ensure that the name is not already registered or trademarked by another company. This can help you avoid legal issues down the road.

5. **Test the name**: Once you have a few potential names, test them out with friends, family, and potential customers to get feedback on which name resonates the most with your target market.

Here are some examples of successful startup brand names and how they reflect the company's identity:

-**Airbnb**: The name "Airbnb" reflects the company's mission of providing affordable and unique accommodations for travelers.

-**Dropbox**: The name "Dropbox" reflects the company's focus on file sharing and storage.

-**Slack**: The name "Slack" reflects the company's mission of providing a communication tool that helps teams work more efficiently.

-**Uber**: The name "Uber" reflects the company's focus on providing a convenient and fast transportation option for customers.

-**Zillow**: The name "Zillow" reflects the company's mission of providing a comprehensive database of real estate information for home buyers and sellers.

Overall, choosing a brand name for your startup requires careful consideration and research. By following these steps and considering successful examples of startup brand names, you can create a strong and memorable brand identity that resonates with your target market.

Step2: Buy your domain

Buying a domain for a startup is an essential step towards building a brand online. Here are the steps you can follow to buy a domain for your startup:

1. Choose a domain registrar: A domain registrar is a company that sells domain names. There are many domain registrars to choose from, such as GoDaddy, Namecheap, and Domain.com. Compare their pricing, features, and customer support before making a decision.

2. Search for available domain names: Use the domain registrar's search tool to check if your desired domain name is available. If it's not available, the tool will suggest alternative options.

3. Choose a domain extension: A domain extension is the last part of a domain name, such as .com, .org, or .net. Choose a domain extension that fits your business needs. For example, .com is the most popular and widely recognized extension, while .org is commonly used for non-profit organizations.

4. Register the domain name: Once you have found an available domain name, select the registration period, add it to your cart, and proceed to checkout. You will need to provide your personal and billing information to complete the registration.

5. Set up DNS: DNS stands for Domain Name System, which connects your domain name to your website hosting provider. You can either use the domain registrar's default DNS or set up your own custom DNS.

Examples:

Let's say your startup is called "ABC Startup" and you want to buy a domain name for your website. Here's an example of how you can buy a domain from Namecheap:

-Go to Namecheap.com and search for "ABC Startup" in the search bar.

-The search tool will show you available domain names with different extensions. You can choose a domain name like abcstartup.com or abcstartup.net.

-Click on the "Add to Cart" button, select the registration period, and proceed to checkout.

-Provide your personal and billing information, and complete the registration process.

-You will receive an email with instructions on how to set up DNS for your domain. You can either use Namecheap's default DNS or set up your custom DNS.

Once you have purchased your domain name, you can use it to create your website and start building your online presence.

Step 3: Create a brand identity

Creating a strong brand identity is crucial for the success of a startup. A brand identity is the visual and emotional representation of a company and its values. It includes the company name, logo, tagline, typography, color palette, and other visual elements that help customers recognize and remember the brand. Here are the steps to create a brand identity for a startup with examples:

1. Define your brand strategy and values:

The first step in creating a brand identity is to define your brand strategy and values. This involves understanding your target audience, unique selling proposition (USP), and overall vision for your brand. It's essential to define your brand values and what your brand stands for, as it will help you create a consistent and compelling brand identity.

For example, Patagonia, a company that produces outdoor clothing and gear, has a strong brand identity that is built on the values of environmentalism and sustainability. Their tagline, "We're in business to save our home planet," reflects their commitment to environmental stewardship.

2. Create a brand name:

Your brand name should be memorable, easy to spell, and reflective of your brand values. You can choose a name that is descriptive of your product or service or create a unique name that is unrelated to your offering.

For example, Tesla, a company that produces electric vehicles, has a brand name that is distinctive and memorable. The name Tesla is inspired by the Serbian-American inventor Nikola Tesla, who is known for his contributions to the development of the modern electrical power system.

3. Design a logo:

Your logo is the visual representation of your brand and should be simple, distinctive, and memorable. It should be designed to reflect your brand values and be easily recognizable across all marketing materials.

For example, Nike's logo, the "swoosh," is a simple and iconic design that has become synonymous with the brand. The logo represents movement and speed, which aligns with the brand's focus on athletic performance.

4. Choose a color palette and typography:

Your brand's color palette and typography should be consistent across all marketing materials. Choose colors that reflect your brand values and create a mood that resonates with your target audience.

For example, Coca-Cola's red and white color palette is instantly recognizable and has become synonymous with the brand. The font used in the logo and marketing materials is unique and distinctive, adding to the brand's overall identity.

5. Develop a tagline:

Your tagline should be memorable and reflect your brand's unique selling proposition. It should communicate your brand values and differentiate your brand from competitors.

For example, Apple's tagline, "Think Different," communicates the brand's focus on innovation and creativity. The tagline is simple and memorable and has become synonymous with the brand.

6. Create a brand style guide:

A brand style guide is a document that outlines the guidelines for using your brand identity across all marketing materials. It includes guidelines for using your logo, color palette, typography, and other visual elements.

For example, Airbnb's brand style guide is comprehensive and outlines guidelines for using their logo, color palette, typography, and photography style. The brand style guide ensures that all marketing materials are consistent and aligned with the brand's values and identity.

Hence, creating a strong brand identity requires a clear understanding of your brand strategy, values, and target audience. By following the steps above, you can create a compelling brand identity that reflects your brand's unique personality and resonates with your target audience.

Step4 : Build your website

Building a website for a startup without investing much money is possible and there are various tools and resources available to help you do so. Here are some steps you can follow to get started:

1. Choose a website builder: There are various website builders available that offer free or low-cost plans. Some of the popular website builders are Wix, Weebly, WordPress, and Squarespace. Choose the one that fits your requirements and budget.

2. Choose a domain name: Your domain name is your website's address. Choose a domain name that is easy to remember and represents your brand. You can use domain name generators such as NameMesh, Nameboy, or Lean Domain Search to find the perfect domain name for your website.

3. Choose a hosting provider: Your hosting provider is where your website is stored and served from. There are many hosting providers available, such as Bluehost, HostGator, and SiteGround. Choose the one that fits your budget and requirements.

4. Choose a template: Once you have chosen your website builder and hosting provider, choose a template for your website. Most website builders offer pre-designed templates that you can customize to your liking.

5. Customize your website: Customize your website by adding your brand's logo, changing colors, and adding content. Make sure your website is easy to navigate and has a clear call to action.

6. Optimize your website for search engines: Optimize your website for search engines by adding meta tags, optimizing your content, and adding relevant keywords.

7. Launch your website: Once you have customized your website and optimized it for search engines, it's time to launch your website. Make sure everything works correctly and test your website thoroughly before going live.

Some tools and resources that can help you build your website include Canva for designing graphics and images, Google Analytics for tracking website performance, and Yoast SEO for optimizing your website for search engines. Once your website is ready, it's time to launch it. Share your website on social media and in your email marketing campaigns. Track your website's analytics to see how well it's performing and make adjustments as needed.

Step5: Test and iterate

Testing and iterating a website for a startup is an important process to ensure that the website is user-friendly, functional, and meets the needs of its target audience. Here are some steps you can follow to test and iterate a website:

1. Establish goals and metrics: The first step in testing and iterating a website is to establish clear goals and metrics that will help you measure the success of the website. For example, you may want to measure the number of visitors, the time spent on the site, the bounce rate, and the conversion rate.

2. Conduct user testing: User testing is an essential part of the website testing process. This involves observing and collecting feedback from users as they navigate through the site. You can use tools like UserTesting or UsabilityHub to conduct remote user testing or recruit users to test the website in person.

3. Analyze data: Once you have collected user feedback and website usage data, analyze it to identify areas that need improvement. You can use tools like Google Analytics to track website metrics and identify patterns in user behavior.

4. Make improvements: Use the feedback and data analysis to make improvements to the website. This could include optimizing the website for mobile devices, improving the navigation and user flow, or making the website more visually appealing.

5. Test again: After making improvements, test the website again to ensure that the changes have had a positive impact. You can repeat this process as many times as necessary to achieve the desired results.

Here are some examples of how you could apply these steps to a startup website:

- A startup that offers an online marketplace for vintage clothing could establish goals such as increasing the number of registered users and the number of items sold per month. They could conduct user testing to identify areas where users may be experiencing difficulties, such as finding specific items or making a purchase. They could then make improvements to the search function, checkout process, and user interface, and test the website again to measure the impact of the changes.

- A startup that offers an online tool for managing social media accounts could establish goals such as increasing the number of users who sign up for a free trial and the number of users who upgrade to a paid subscription. They could conduct user testing to identify areas where users may be confused or frustrated, such as setting up a new social media account. They could then make improvements to the onboarding process, user interface, and support resources, and test the website again to measure the impact of the changes.

By following these steps, you can create a basic prototype for your brand and website. Remember to stay focused on your target audience and continuously improve your brand and website to better serve them.

Showcase prototype using a video

I understand developing a product or platform needs a lot of funds and founders at early stage lack those funds and hence do not get a chance to test their idea or create prototypes.

Stop waiting for funds or delay your fund raise processes to start working on your idea!

Using a video as a prototype for a product demo can be an effective way to showcase the features and functionality of a product to potential customers or investors. Here are some key benefits and considerations:

<u>**Benefits:**</u>

- **Visual representation:** Videos can help to visually demonstrate how a product works and highlight its key features, which can be more engaging than simply reading or hearing about them.

- **Accessibility:** Videos can be shared easily online and accessed by anyone with an internet connection, which can help to reach a wider audience than an in-person demo.

- **Reproducibility:** A video demo can be recorded once and shared multiple times, which can save time and resources compared to conducting in-person demos each time.

- **Flexibility:** Videos can be edited and refined as needed to showcase the product in the best possible way.

<u>**Considerations:**</u>

- **Accuracy:** It's important to ensure that the video accurately represents the product and its features, as misrepresentations could lead to confusion or disappointment for potential customers.

- **Production quality:** The quality of the video can impact how the product is perceived, so it's important to invest in high-quality video production if possible.

- **Length:** Attention spans can be short, so it's important to keep the video concise and focused on the most important features of the product.

- **Context:** While a video demo can be effective, it may not be appropriate for all products or audiences. Consider the context in which the product will be used and the preferences of the target audience when deciding whether a video demo is the best approach.

Hence, using a video as a prototype for a product demo can be an effective way to showcase a product's features and functionality, but it's important to carefully consider the benefits and drawbacks before deciding whether it's the best approach.

Minimum Viable Product (MVP)

A minimum viable product, or MVP, is a product with enough features to attract early-adopter customers and validate a product idea early in the product development cycle. In industries such as software, the MVP can help the product team receive user feedback as quickly as possible to iterate and improve the product.

Because the agile methodology is built on validating and iterating products based on user input, the MVP plays a central role in agile development.

The idea is to get feedback from the consumers which will in turn help in making the desired changes in the final product. MVP actually tests the usage scenario rather that is much for more helpful for the company to make changes to the final product.

Let's understand the concept with the help of an example: MVP is a popular concept in the online space, where a website is launched with basic features to find out how consumers respond to the product displayed on the website.

It could be a consumable product, daily use product or even a service provided by a website provider. The idea is to start small and then take cues from the users as to what exactly are they expecting from the product.

Some of the noted examples are Dropbox, Groupon, Zappos, etc.

What is the purpose of building MVPs?

The primary goal of the MVP is to always minimize time and effort wasted by testing how the market reacts to your idea before building the complete product.

As a product manager, MVPs can help you

- Validate product idea hypotheses with real-life data.
- Reduce time-to-market for new feature releases.
- Deliver value to your early adopters quickly.

The MVP is the shortest route that delivers the most value to your first customers while simultaneously generating learnings for you. Test your product/market fit before building a full-fledged product.

Collect viable data on user behavior to shape future product initiatives and go-to-market strategy. MVPs can be used as a leading component in your product prioritization process to help you make data-driven decisions.

- Grow a pre-launch user base.
- Eliminate waste — save money and time that would otherwise be spent on fruitless ideas

Examples of Minimum Viable Products from top tech companies

- **Dropbox**

Instead of building a full-fledged solution that would require overcoming extreme technical hurdles and months of development, Drew Houston (one of the co-founders of Dropbox), created a simple three-minute video demonstration of the technology. Targeted at high-tech adopters, the video explained how easy it is to use the file-sharing platform.

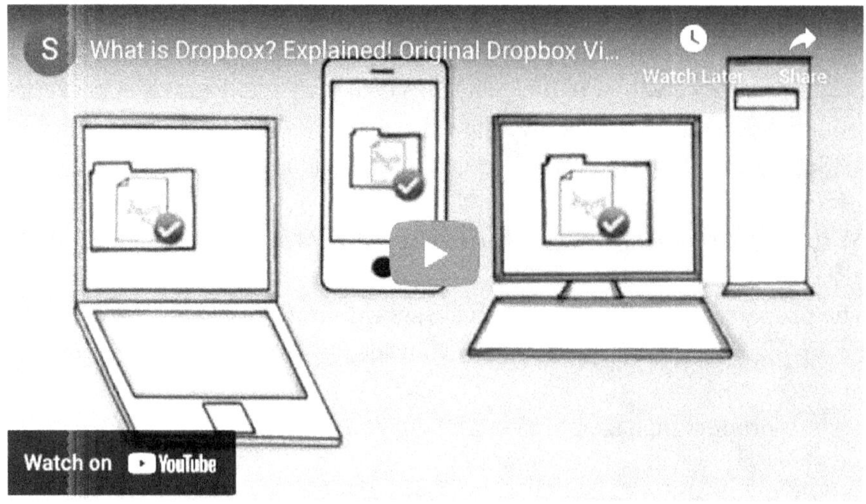

The video led to 75,000 people waiting for a beta invite, literally overnight. Today, Dropbox is rumored to be worth more than $10 billion.

In the case of Dropbox, Houston used a video as a minimum viable product to validate his hypothesis that people wanted a file-sharing software that "just works like magic". The flocks of people signing up successfully validated his hypothesis.

- **Facebook**

It's hard to imagine that social media juggernaut Facebook was once a website with the sole purpose of connecting students at Harvard University. Thefacebook (Facebook's MVP!), as it was then called, was a simple platform that connected students from the same classes by allowing them to post messages to shared boards.

By introducing Facebook to a super-narrow segment of the market, Zuckerberg managed to validate his idea and gain critical mass that later skyrocketed the adoption of the social media network. We all know how the story ends.

MVP Vs Prototype

MVP and prototype are two terms that are often used interchangeably, but they actually refer to two distinct concepts in product development.

- MVP stands for Minimum Viable Product, which is a basic version of a product that has just enough features to satisfy early customers and to validate a product idea. It is a fully functional product that is designed to address the core problem of the target audience. The goal of an MVP is to get feedback from early adopters and use that feedback to iterate and improve the product over time. MVPs are typically used in startups and new product development where the goal is to quickly test and validate a product idea with minimal resources.

- A prototype, on the other hand, is a preliminary version of a product that is designed to test specific aspects of the product's functionality or design. It can be a physical or digital model that is used to demonstrate how the product will work and to gather feedback on the user experience. Prototypes are typically used in more established companies or product development cycles to test out new features or to make design improvements.

In summary, an MVP is a fully functional product that is designed to address the core problem of the target audience and to get feedback from early adopters, while a prototype is a preliminary version of a product that is designed to test specific aspects of the product's functionality or design.

Proof of Concept

Proof of concept refers to a demonstration that shows the feasibility and potential of a particular idea, product, or concept. It is a preliminary stage in the development of a new technology, process, or product, where the primary focus is to validate the fundamental principles of the concept, rather than its commercial viability.

The proof of concept is usually created by creating a prototype or a mock-up of the product or technology. This prototype is used to test the concept and to identify any potential issues or problems that may arise during the development process. Once the proof of concept has been successfully tested, it can be used to generate interest, secure funding, or attract investment from potential stakeholders.

The main purpose of a proof of concept is to demonstrate that the idea or concept is viable and feasible. It is also used to identify any potential issues or challenges that may arise during the development process. By addressing these issues early on, it is possible to avoid costly mistakes and ensure that the final product or technology is of high quality.

Benefits of Proof of Concept

Now investors prefer funding in startups that at least have a map or any proof of concepts. Why?
Proof of concept (POC) is a crucial step in the product development process, particularly in technology-based projects. It is essentially a small-scale version of the final product that is created to test and validate the feasibility of the concept or idea.

- POC is important because it helps to identify potential problems or issues that might arise when developing the final product. By creating a prototype or a small-scale model, you can test the functionality of the product, evaluate its market potential, and determine if it's worth investing further resources into the development of the final product.

- POC also helps to minimize risks and costs associated with product development. By testing the concept before investing significant resources, you can identify flaws in the design or functionality and make changes before committing to a full-scale development effort. This can save time, money, and resources, and help to ensure the final product meets user needs and expectations.

Hence, POC is an important step in the product development process that helps to identify potential issues, minimize risks, and validate the feasibility of the concept before investing significant resources into the development of the final product.

Steps to POC

Here are some general steps that can be followed to prove the concept:
1. Define the concept: Start by defining the concept you want to prove. Clearly articulate what the concept is, what problem it solves, and what

benefits it provides.

2. Identify the goals: Define the goals of the proof of concept. What do you want to achieve? What questions do you want to answer? What metrics will be used to measure success?

3. Develop a plan: Develop a plan for executing the proof of concept. This plan should outline the steps that will be taken, the resources required, and the timeline for completion.

4. Build a prototype: Build a prototype or a mock-up of the product or technology. This prototype should be functional enough to demonstrate the concept.

5. Test the concept: Test the prototype to determine whether the concept is feasible and meets the goals of the proof of concept. Collect data and feedback from users and stakeholders to assess the success of the proof of concept.

6. Analyze the results: Analyze the results of the testing to identify any issues or challenges that need to be addressed. Use this feedback to refine the concept and improve the prototype.

7. Evaluate the feasibility: Evaluate the feasibility of the concept based on the results of the testing. Determine whether the concept is viable and whether it can be developed into a successful product or technology.

8. Communicate the results: Communicate the results of the proof of concept to stakeholders, investors, and potential users. Use this communication to generate interest and secure funding for further development.

9. Refine the concept: Use the feedback and data collected during the proof of concept to refine the concept and improve the prototype. Iterate through the process until the concept is fully developed and ready for commercialization.

By following these steps, you can prove the concept and develop a successful product or technology that meets the needs of its intended users.

Lets take an example:

An example of a proof of concept could be the development of a new mobile application. Here are the steps involved in this proof of concept:

- Define the concept: The concept is a new mobile application that provides users with a platform to find and book local fitness classes.

- Identify the goals: The goals of the proof of concept are to determine whether users find the app useful, whether they are able to find and book classes easily, and whether the app has potential for further development and investment.

- Develop a plan: The plan is to develop a functional prototype of the app and to test it with a small group of users over a period of two weeks.

- Build a prototype: The prototype is a functional mobile application that includes a searchable database of local fitness classes, booking functionality, and user profiles.

- Test the concept: The prototype is tested with a group of ten users who use the app to find and book fitness classes. Data and feedback are collected from the users throughout the testing period.

- Analyze the results: The results show that the users find the app useful and easy to use. However, some issues are identified with the booking functionality, which is refined based on user feedback.

- Evaluate the feasibility: Based on the results of the testing, it is determined that the concept is feasible and has potential for further development.

- Communicate the results: The results are communicated to potential investors and stakeholders to generate interest and secure funding for further development.

- Refine the concept: The concept is refined based on user feedback and further developed into a fully functional mobile application that is launched to the public.

In this example, the proof of concept helped to validate the feasibility of the new mobile application and identify areas for improvement. It also provided valuable feedback for further development and investment.

Challenges while doing Proof of concept

There can be various challenges while doing a Proof of Concept (PoC), depending on the nature of the project and the specific goals of the PoC. However, here are some common challenges that are often encountered during the PoC phase:

- **Defining the problem:** The first and foremost challenge is to clearly define the problem statement and set the scope of the PoC. This requires a clear understanding of the business requirements and objectives, and an accurate assessment of the technology landscape.

- **Data availability:** A PoC requires access to data, which can be a major challenge in many cases. It may require additional resources or technology to collect and analyze the required data, and there may be legal and ethical constraints that need to be considered.

-**Time constraints:** A PoC is typically a time-bound activity, and there may be a limited amount of time available to complete it. This can put pressure on the team to deliver results quickly, which can sometimes compromise the quality of the work.

- **Resource constraints:** The availability of skilled resources, such as data scientists and software engineers, can be a challenge during the PoC phase. There may also be limitations in terms of technology infrastructure and computing resources.

- **Technical complexity:** Depending on the nature of the project, the technical complexity of the PoC can be a challenge. This can include the need for specialized knowledge or expertise, as well as the need to integrate different systems and technologies.

- **Measuring success:** It can be challenging to define success criteria for a PoC, especially when dealing with emerging technologies or complex business problems. This can make it difficult to measure the effectiveness of the PoC and assess its impact on the business.

- **Managing expectations:** There may be high expectations for the PoC, especially if it is seen as a key milestone in a larger project. Managing these expectations and communicating the limitations and uncertainties of the PoC can be a challenge, but is essential for ensuring that the project remains on track.

Why investors ask for proof of concept?

Investors ask for proof of concept (PoC) to evaluate the feasibility of a business idea or technology before investing their money. PoC is an important step in the early stages of a startup, as it demonstrates that the idea or technology is viable, and has the potential to solve a real-world problem.

Here are a few reasons why investors ask for proof of concept:

1. **Risk mitigation:** Investing in a startup is inherently risky, and investors want to minimize that risk as much as possible. A well-executed PoC demonstrates that the idea or technology has been thoroughly tested, reducing the risk of failure in the future.

2. **Market validation:** A PoC can help to validate the market potential of a product or service. By demonstrating that there is a real need for the idea or technology, investors can be more confident that there is a market for the product or service.

3. **Technical feasibility:** Investors want to ensure that the technology behind the idea is feasible and can be developed into a working product or service. A successful PoC provides evidence that the technology works as intended and can be scaled up to meet demand.

4. **Business model validation:** A PoC can help to validate the business model behind the startup. It provides evidence that the idea or technology can generate revenue and profits, and that there is a viable path to market.

A successful PoC can provide investors with the confidence they need to invest in a startup. It demonstrates that the idea or technology has been thoroughly tested, validated, and has the potential for success in the market.

Proof of concept is nothing without analytics

Analytics play a critical role in measuring the success of a Proof of Concept (PoC). The main purpose of analytics in a PoC is to provide data-driven insights into the performance of the idea or technology being tested, as well as the effectiveness of the PoC itself. Here are some of the key analytics that are often measured during a PoC:

- **User engagement:** Analytics can be used to measure user engagement with the idea or technology being tested. This includes metrics such as the number of users, frequency of usage, and duration of usage. By tracking user engagement, it is possible to assess the viability of the idea or technology in the market.

- **Conversion rates:** Analytics can be used to measure the conversion rates of users, such as the percentage of users who sign up for a service, make a purchase, or complete a desired action. This can provide insight into the effectiveness of the product or service being tested, as well as the user experience.

- **Performance metrics:** Analytics can be used to measure the performance of the idea or technology being tested, such as the speed, reliability, and scalability of the system. This can provide insight into the technical feasibility of the product or service.

- **Financial metrics:** Analytics can be used to measure financial metrics such as revenue, costs, and profits. This can help to validate the business model behind the idea or technology being tested, and provide insight into the potential for long-term profitability.

- **Customer feedback:** Analytics can be used to measure customer feedback, such as ratings, reviews, and user surveys. This can provide valuable insights into the user experience, as well as identify areas for improvement.

Hence, analytics play a critical role in measuring the success of a PoC. By tracking key metrics and analyzing data, it is possible to assess the viability of the idea or technology being tested, and make data-driven decisions about its future development.

Here's an example of a proof of concept with analytics:

Suppose a company wants to improve their online customer experience by implementing a chatbot on their website. Before investing in a full-scale implementation, they decide to do a proof of concept to determine whether the chatbot will be effective in improving customer satisfaction and reducing support costs.

To conduct the proof of concept, the company implements a simple chatbot on their website and collects data on how customers interact with it. They use analytics to track metrics such as:

- **Conversation duration:** How long customers spend interacting with the chatbot.

- **Customer satisfaction:** How satisfied customers are with the chatbot's responses.

- **Issue resolution rate:** The percentage of customer issues that are resolved by the chatbot.

- **Support cost savings:** The cost savings resulting from the chatbot resolving issues that would otherwise require human support.

Using these metrics, the company can evaluate whether the chatbot is effective in improving the customer experience and reducing support costs. If the proof of concept is successful, the company can then move forward with a full-scale implementation of the chatbot.

Conducting a proof of concept with analytics allows the company to make an informed decision about whether to invest in a new technology or strategy. By collecting and analyzing data, the company can identify potential benefits and drawbacks and make a more informed decision about whether to move forward with the project.

How to reach potential customers for proof of concept?

When conducting a proof of concept, it is important to reach potential customers to gather feedback and validate your idea. Here are some ways to reach potential customers for a proof of concept:

1. Tap into your existing network: Reach out to your current customers, industry peers, and business contacts to see if they are interested in testing your product or service. They may be able to provide valuable feedback and insights.

2. Utilize social media: Social media platforms such as LinkedIn, Twitter, and Facebook can be effective for reaching potential customers. Use targeted ads and posts to reach your desired audience and encourage them to participate in your proof of concept.

3. Attend industry events: Attend industry events and conferences where your potential customers are likely to be. This is a great way to network with potential customers and generate interest in your proof of concept.

4. Partner with industry influencers: Partner with influencers in your industry who have a large following and can help promote your proof of concept to their audience.

5. Offer incentives: Offer incentives such as free trials or discounts to encourage potential customers to participate in your proof of concept.

6. Leverage email marketing: Use email marketing to reach potential customers who have opted in to receive your communications. Personalize your emails and include a clear call to action to encourage them to participate in your proof of concept.

By utilizing these methods, you can reach potential customers and gather feedback on your proof of concept, which can help you improve your product or service and make it more appealing to your target audience.

How to build a business or revenue model

One of the most important aspects of starting a business is creating a sustainable revenue model. It is the foundation upon which the startup will grow, expand and generate revenue. The business model outlines how the startup plans to generate revenue, who the target audience is, and how they plan to reach them. In this chapter, we will discuss how to build a business or revenue model for a startup.

Identify your target audience

The first step in building a business or revenue model is to identify your target audience. This will help you understand who your customers are, what they need, and how you can reach them. You should conduct thorough market research to identify your target audience, including their age, gender, location, income, interests, and preferences.

For example, if your startup is in the beauty industry, you may target women aged 18-35 who are interested in makeup and skincare.

Determine your revenue streams

Once you have identified your target audience, you need to determine how you will generate revenue. There are various revenue models to choose from, including:

1. Direct Sales Model: This model is based on selling products or services directly to customers through different channels. For example, e-commerce websites like Amazon and Shopify operate under this model.

2. **Advertising Model:** This model is based on generating revenue by selling advertising space on websites or apps. Social media platforms like Facebook and Instagram are examples of advertising-based startups.

3. **Subscription Model:** This model is based on charging customers a recurring fee for access to a product or service. Companies like Netflix and Spotify operate under this model.

4. **Freemium Model:** This model is based on offering a basic version of a product or service for free and charging customers for premium features. Companies like Dropbox and LinkedIn operate under this model.

For example, if your startup is a beauty subscription box, you may use a subscription model where customers pay a monthly fee to receive a box of beauty products.

While deciding on the revenue model, it's essential to consider factors such as the target audience, competition, and pricing strategies.

Here are some ways you should use to build a sustainable revenue model for your startup:

Determine your pricing strategy

Determining a pricing strategy for a startup can be a challenging task as there are various factors to consider such as the target market, competition, production costs, and revenue goals. Here are the steps you can follow to determine a pricing strategy for a startup along with a use case example:

-**Identify the target market:** The first step in determining the pricing strategy is to identify the target market. Start by defining the characteristics of your target audience, such as demographics, needs, and preferences. This will help you understand their willingness to pay for your product or service.

For example, let's consider a startup that provides an online tutoring service for high school students. The target market for this startup would be parents who are looking for affordable and effective tutoring services for their children.

-**Research your competition**: Once you have identified your target market, the next step is to research your competition. Analyze the pricing strategies of your competitors and evaluate their strengths and weaknesses.

For instance, in the case of the online tutoring service startup, there are several competitors in the market that offer similar services. The startup can research the pricing models of these competitors and see how they are positioning their products to attract customers.

-**Determine your production costs:** The next step is to determine your production costs, including materials, labor, and overhead costs. This will give you a baseline for how much you need to charge to break even and make a profit.

Continuing with the example of the online tutoring startup, the production costs could include expenses related to developing the platform, paying the tutors, and marketing the service.

-**Determine your revenue goals:** Once you have a clear understanding of your production costs, you need to determine your revenue goals. This involves setting a pricing strategy that allows you to meet your financial objectives while remaining competitive in the market.

For the online tutoring service startup, the revenue goal could be to reach a certain number of customers within a specific period. To achieve this, the startup might set a pricing strategy that is competitive with the market, yet allows for enough profit margin to achieve the revenue goal.

-**Choose your pricing strategy:** Based on your research and analysis, you can choose a pricing strategy that aligns with your business goals and meets the needs of your target market. Common pricing strategies include value-based pricing, cost-plus pricing, penetration pricing, and skimming pricing.

For the online tutoring startup, a value-based pricing strategy may be appropriate as the service offers a unique value proposition to parents and students. The startup can analyze the needs and preferences of its target market and set a price that reflects the value of its service.

In conclusion, determining a pricing strategy for a startup requires a thorough understanding of the target market, competition, production costs, revenue goals, and pricing strategies. By following these steps and evaluating the example use case, you can create a pricing strategy that enables your startup to succeed in the market.

Determine your distribution channels

Determining the distribution channels for a startup involves identifying the channels that will be used to get the product or service to customers. Here are the steps you can take to determine the distribution channels for your startup:

- **Define your target audience:** Before you can determine your distribution channels, you need to identify your target audience. Who are your ideal customers? What are their needs, preferences, and buying behaviors?

- **Identify potential distribution channels:** Once you have a clear understanding of your target audience, you can start identifying potential distribution channels. There are several types of distribution channels, including:

- **Direct sales:** Selling directly to customers through your own website or physical store.

- **Retail sales:** Selling your products through retail stores or e-commerce platforms such as Amazon or eBay.

- **Wholesale sales:** Selling your products in bulk to retailers or distributors who then sell them to end customers.

- **Affiliate marketing:** Partnering with other businesses or individuals who promote your products and receive a commission for each sale.

- **Social media:** Using social media platforms such as Instagram, Facebook, or TikTok to promote and sell your products.

- **Referral marketing:** Encouraging existing customers to refer their friends and family to your business.

- **Evaluate each channel:** Once you have identified potential distribution channels, you need to evaluate each channel's potential effectiveness in reaching your target audience. Consider factors such as cost, reach, and the level of control you have over the customer experience.

- **Test and iterate:** After selecting your distribution channels, it's important to test them and make adjustments as needed. Monitor the performance of each channel and make changes to improve the effectiveness of your distribution strategy.

Examples of distribution channels for startups:

- Dollar Shave Club: Dollar Shave Club uses a subscription-based direct sales model to deliver razors and grooming products to customers' doors. Customers can sign up for a subscription online, and products are shipped directly to them on a regular basis.

- Warby Parker: Warby Parker is an eyewear company that sells its products both online and through its physical retail stores. Customers can try on glasses in-store or order them online, and the company offers free shipping and returns.

- Glossier: Glossier is a beauty brand that has built a loyal following through social media marketing. The company sells its products online and through pop-up shops, and relies heavily on user-generated content and influencer marketing to drive sales.

- Airbnb: Airbnb is a platform that connects travelers with hosts who have spare rooms or homes to rent. The company uses a digital platform to facilitate bookings and payments, and has built a strong brand through word-of-mouth marketing and user reviews.

- Harry's: Harry's is another razor and grooming products company that uses a combination of direct sales and retail partnerships to reach customers. The company sells its products online and through retail partnerships with stores such as Target and Walmart.

Determine your customer acquisition strategy

Determining a customer acquisition strategy for a startup involves several steps, including identifying the target audience, defining the value proposition, selecting the most effective channels, and setting a budget. Here are the detailed steps:

1. **Identify the target audience:** Determine the ideal customer profile by understanding their needs, preferences, demographics, and behavior. This will help in tailoring the marketing message and reaching out to the right people.
2. **Define the value proposition:** Articulate the unique selling point (USP) or value proposition that sets the startup apart from the competition. This will help in communicating the benefits of the product or service and convincing customers to make a purchase.
3. **Select the most effective channels:** Choose the marketing channels that align with the target audience and the value proposition. Some examples of channels include social media advertising, search engine optimization, content marketing, email marketing, and influencer marketing.
4. **Set a budget:** Determine how much money can be allocated for customer acquisition, considering the cost of different channels, the conversion rate, and the expected revenue per customer.

5. **Test and refine:** Experiment with different channels and tactics, measure the results, and refine the strategy based on the feedback.

Calculating the cost of customer acquisition (CAC) involves dividing the total cost of sales and marketing by the number of new customers acquired in a given period. Here's the formula:

CAC = Total sales and marketing cost / Number of new customers acquired

For example, if a startup spent $10,000 on sales and marketing in a month and acquired 100 new customers, the CAC would be $100.

Here's another example:

Suppose a startup spent $50,000 on sales and marketing in a year and acquired 500 new customers. The CAC would be:

CAC = $50,000 / 500 = $100

This means that the startup spent $100 on average to acquire each new customer. The CAC can be compared with the customer lifetime value (CLV) to determine the profitability of the business. If the CAC is higher than the CLV, it may indicate that the startup needs to improve its customer retention or reduce its acquisition costs.

Determine your cost structure

Determining the cost structure in a startup is a critical task for any entrepreneur. A cost structure is the framework that outlines all the costs that a company may incur in order to produce and sell its products or services. The following are the steps you can take to determine the cost structure of a startup, along with some examples:

1. **Identify the key cost drivers:** The first step in determining the cost structure of a startup is to identify the key cost drivers. These are the factors that will have the greatest impact on the overall cost of the startup. Some examples of key cost drivers include raw materials, labor, rent, and marketing expenses.

2. **Categorize the costs:** Once you have identified the key cost drivers, categorize the costs into fixed costs and variable costs. Fixed costs are expenses that do not change regardless of the level of production or sales, such as rent or salaries. Variable costs, on the other hand, are expenses that change depending on the level of production or sales, such

as raw materials or sales commissions.

3. **Calculate the break-even point**: The next step is to calculate the break-even point, which is the point at which the revenue generated by the startup equals the total costs. This calculation will help you determine how many units of your product or service you need to sell in order to cover all your costs.

4. **Determine the pricing strategy**: After calculating the break-even point, determine the pricing strategy that will allow you to cover your costs while still remaining competitive in the market.

5. **Monitor and adjust the cost structure**: Finally, monitor your cost structure regularly and make adjustments as necessary. This will help you stay on track and ensure that your startup remains profitable.

Here are some examples of cost structures for different types of startups:

-**E-commerce startup**: A typical cost structure for an e-commerce startup might include fixed costs such as website hosting and development, office rent, and salaries. Variable costs might include payment processing fees, shipping and handling costs, and marketing expenses.

-**Software-as-a-Service (SaaS) startup**: A SaaS startup's cost structure might include fixed costs such as server hosting and salaries, while variable costs might include customer acquisition costs and the cost of providing customer support.

-**Manufacturing startup**: A manufacturing startup's cost structure might include fixed costs such as rent and equipment maintenance, while variable costs might include raw materials, labor, and shipping costs.

-**Service-based startup**: A service-based startup's cost structure might include fixed costs such as office rent and salaries, while variable costs might include the cost of materials and transportation to the job site.

Determine your key metrics

Determining key metrics to measure the success of a startup can vary depending on the industry, stage of the startup, and business model. However, here are some general key metrics that can be useful to measure the success of a startup:

- **Monthly Recurring Revenue (MRR)**: MRR is a critical metric for any subscription-based business model as it helps track the revenue generated by the startup every month. It helps to understand if the business is growing, and if so, at what rate.

- **Customer Acquisition Cost (CAC)**: CAC is the cost incurred by a startup to acquire a new customer. It helps to evaluate the effectiveness of the startup's marketing and sales strategy. Lowering the CAC while maintaining a high-quality customer base is critical for long-term success.

- **Churn Rate:** Churn rate refers to the number of customers who stop using a startup's product or service over a given period. It helps to understand customer loyalty and the overall health of the business. A high churn rate can indicate a problem with the product or service, customer support, or pricing.

- **Gross Margin**: Gross margin is the difference between the revenue generated by a product or service and the cost of producing and delivering it. A higher gross margin indicates that the startup is generating more profit for every dollar of revenue.

- **User Engagement:** User engagement metrics, such as daily or monthly active users, session duration, and retention rate, help understand how users interact with a startup's product or service. It can help to identify what features or aspects of the product are working well and which ones need improvement.

- **Runway:** Runway refers to the amount of time a startup can operate before running out of cash. It is essential to track and manage the startup's cash flow to ensure its survival.

- **Net Promoter Score (NPS):** NPS is a measure of customer satisfaction and loyalty. It helps to understand how likely a customer is to recommend a startup's product or service to others. A higher NPS indicates that customers are more likely to recommend the product or service to others, which can lead to more growth and revenue.

Examples of these key metrics in action include:

-A SaaS startup that tracks its MRR to ensure that its subscription revenue is growing at a healthy rate.

-An e-commerce startup that tracks its CAC to ensure that its marketing and sales strategy is cost-effective.

-A mobile app startup that tracks its churn rate to identify and address any product or customer support issues.

-A hardware startup that tracks its gross margin to ensure that it is generating enough profit to cover its production and delivery costs.

-A social media startup that tracks user engagement to identify the most popular features and improve user experience.

-A pre-seed startup that tracks its runway to ensure that it has enough cash to continue operating until it can secure more funding.

-A consumer goods startup that tracks its NPS to identify satisfied customers who are likely to recommend its products to others.

In conclusion, building a business or revenue model for a startup is critical to its success. It involves identifying your target audience, determining your revenue streams, pricing strategy, distribution channels, customer acquisition strategy, cost structure, and key metrics. By following these steps and constantly evaluating and adjusting your model, you can build a successful.

CHAPTER EIGHT

How to build a right team?

Building the right team for a startup in its early stages is crucial for its success. A strong team can bring together a range of skills and expertise, and work collaboratively towards a shared goal. A team that is passionate, committed, and works well together can help to drive innovation, solve problems, and overcome challenges. Conversely, a team that lacks the necessary skills, motivation, or cohesion can hinder progress and impact the success of the startup. So, it's important to invest time and effort in building the right team for your startup.

Define your startup's mission and vision:

Defining a clear mission and vision for your startup is crucial for attracting and hiring the right team members. A mission statement is a concise statement that outlines the purpose and goals of your startup. A vision statement is a long-term view of what your startup wants to achieve in the future. Here's how to define your startup's mission and vision for hiring a team, with examples:

Define your startup's mission:

Your mission statement should be a clear and concise statement that describes your startup's purpose and what you hope to achieve.

Start by answering the following questions:

- What problem does your startup solve?
- Who does your startup serve?
- What values are important to your startup?

Example:

Our mission at XYZ Inc. is to provide affordable and accessible healthcare to underserved communities. We believe that everyone deserves access to quality healthcare, and we strive to make that a reality by leveraging technology and innovative solutions.

-Define your startup's vision:

Your vision statement should describe your startup's long-term goals and what you hope to achieve in the future. Start by answering the following questions:

- Where do you see your startup in 5, 10, or 20 years?
- What is the ultimate goal of your startup?
- What impact do you want to make in the world?

Example:

Our vision at XYZ Inc. is to become the leading provider of telemedicine services in the world, and to ensure that everyone has access to quality healthcare, regardless of their location or financial situation. We believe that technology can revolutionize healthcare, and we are committed to creating a world where everyone has access to the care they need.

Use your mission and vision to attract and hire the right team members:

Once you have defined your startup's mission and vision, use them to attract and hire team members who share your values and goals. Be sure to communicate your mission and vision clearly in your job postings, and ask candidates how they align with your startup's mission and vision during the interview process.

Example job posting:

We are looking for a passionate and dedicated software engineer to join our team at XYZ Inc. Our mission is to provide affordable and accessible healthcare to underserved communities, and our vision is to become the leading provider of telemedicine services in the world. If you share our values and are committed to using technology to revolutionize healthcare, we want to hear from you!

In summary, defining a clear mission and vision for your startup is critical for attracting and hiring the right team members. By communicating your mission and vision in your job postings and during the interview process, you can attract team members who share your values and are committed to helping you achieve your goals.

Look for passion and enthusiasm:

When hiring a team for a startup, it's important to look for individuals who not only possess the necessary skills and experience but also demonstrate passion and enthusiasm for the company's mission and vision. Here are some ways to identify passion and enthusiasm in potential team members:

- **Look for individuals who have pursued similar interests outside of work:** For example, if your startup is focused on sustainability, look for candidates who have shown interest in environmental activism, volunteered for conservation efforts or participated in community gardening.

- **Ask candidates about their career goals:** Passionate individuals are more likely to have clear and ambitious career goals. Listen for signs that the candidate has thought about how your startup could help them achieve their career aspirations.

- **Look for examples of creativity and innovation:** Passionate individuals tend to be more creative and innovative. Ask candidates about times when they have developed new processes or implemented new ideas.

- **Check for industry knowledge:** Passionate individuals tend to be more knowledgeable about the industry they work in. Ask candidates about trends and challenges they see in your industry and how they would address them.

- **Look for excitement during the interview:** Pay attention to the candidate's tone of voice, body language and overall energy level during the interview. Candidates who are passionate about your startup will likely show excitement and enthusiasm during the interview.

Examples of questions to ask during the interview to assess passion and enthusiasm:

-What motivated you to apply for this position?

-What are you most excited about in regards to this company?

-What has been your biggest accomplishment in your career so far?

-How do you keep up to date with industry trends and developments?

-How have you applied creativity or innovation in your past roles?

-How do you see your career aligning with the goals of this startup?

By assessing passion and enthusiasm during the hiring process, you can build a team that is not only skilled but also dedicated and invested in your startup's success.

Identify the roles you need to fill

Identifying the roles you need to fill for hiring a team for a startup can be a challenging task, but it's crucial to get it right to ensure the success of your company. Below are some steps you can take to identify the roles you need to fill:

1. **Start with your business plan:** Your business plan should give you a good idea of the areas of your business that will require specific expertise. For example, if you plan to develop a mobile app, you'll likely need developers, designers, and possibly a project manager.

2. **Determine the skills and experience required:** Once you have identified the areas of your business that require specific expertise, you need to determine the skills and experience required for each role. For example, if you need a developer, you may require expertise in a particular programming language or experience in developing mobile apps.

3. **Prioritize the roles:** After identifying the required skills and experience, prioritize the roles based on their importance to your business. For example, a developer may be more critical to your business than a marketing specialist, depending on your business's nature.

4. **Consider the size of your startup:** If you are a small startup, you may not have the budget to hire a full team for each role. In this case, you may need to identify roles that can be combined or filled by one person.

5. **Look at your competition:** Look at your competition and see what roles they have filled. This can give you an idea of the roles that are critical for your business.

Examples of roles to consider for a startup team:

-CEO: Responsible for the overall strategy and direction of the company.

-CTO: Responsible for the company's technology strategy and development.

-COO: Responsible for the day-to-day operations of the company.

-Project Manager: Responsible for overseeing the development of specific projects.

-Developer: Responsible for developing and maintaining the company's software and/or website.

-Designer: Responsible for creating the visual design of the company's products.

-Marketing Specialist: Responsible for developing and executing the company's marketing strategy.

-Sales Representative: Responsible for selling the company's products or services to customers.

-Customer Service Representative: Responsible for providing support to customers.

-Finance Specialist: Responsible for managing the company's finances, including budgeting and accounting.

Overall, the roles you need to fill for your startup team will depend on your business's nature, size, and goals. It's essential to take the time to identify the roles you need to fill and to prioritize them to ensure your team's success.

Look for candidates with relevant skills and experience

Looking for candidates with relevant skills and experience for a startup can be a challenging task, but there are several effective strategies that can help you identify the best candidates. Here are some steps you can take:

1. **Define your hiring needs:** Before you start looking for candidates, it's important to define your hiring needs. What positions do you need to fill? What specific skills and experience are required for each position? What type of culture do you want to foster in your startup? Once you have a clear idea of what you're looking for, you can start targeting your search.

2. **Use multiple sourcing channels:** There are several channels you can use to find candidates, including job boards, social media, referrals, networking events, and recruitment agencies. Using multiple channels will increase your chances of finding the right candidates.

3. **Create a job description that stands out:** Your job description should clearly outline the role, responsibilities, and requirements for the position. But it should also be compelling and highlight why working for your startup is unique and exciting. Use language that reflects your company culture and values to attract candidates who align with those ideals.

4. **Screen resumes and cover letters:** When reviewing resumes and cover letters, look for candidates who have relevant experience and skills. Pay attention to any gaps in employment or inconsistencies in their work history. You can also use software to help you screen resumes and filter out candidates who don't meet your criteria.

5. **Conduct thorough interviews:** During the interview process, ask questions that relate to the candidate's experience and skills. Ask about

specific projects they've worked on, their approach to problem-solving, and how they've handled difficult situations. Use behavioral interview questions to get a better sense of how they would fit into your startup culture.

6. Consider work samples and assessments: Depending on the position, you may want to ask candidates to complete a work sample or assessment to demonstrate their skills. This can be particularly helpful for technical roles or positions that require specific certifications or qualifications.

7. Check references: Always check a candidate's references before making an offer. Ask their former employers or colleagues about their work ethic, communication skills, and how they handle challenges.

Examples:

Let's say you're looking for a software engineer for your startup. Here are some examples of how you can use the above strategies to find the right candidate:

-Define your hiring needs: You need a software engineer who has experience with full-stack development, can work independently, and is comfortable with agile methodologies.

-Use multiple sourcing channels: Post the job on job boards, reach out to software development communities on social media, attend networking events for developers, and work with a recruitment agency.

-Create a job description that stands out: Your job description should include details about the technologies you use, the type of projects the engineer will work on, and the company culture. Highlight your startup's unique mission and values.

-Screen resumes and cover letters: Look for candidates who have experience with the specific technologies you use and have worked on projects similar to what you're building. Pay attention to any gaps in employment or frequent job changes.

-Conduct thorough interviews: Ask questions about their experience with full-stack development, how they approach problem-solving, and their experience working in an agile environment. Use behavioral interview questions to assess their communication skills and teamwork abilities.

-Consider work samples and assessments: Ask candidates to complete a coding challenge that demonstrates their skills and approach to problem-solving.

-Check references: Speak with the candidate's former colleagues and supervisors to learn more about their work ethic, communication skills, and how they handle pressure.

Evaluate candidates' cultural fit:

Evaluating a candidate's cultural fit for a startup is crucial for ensuring that they align with the company's values, goals, and working environment. Here are some steps and examples that can help you evaluate a candidate's cultural fit in detail:

1. **Define the company culture**: Start by defining the company culture and its values. Consider what makes your startup unique, what kind of work environment you have, and what values and goals the company holds. For example, if your startup values innovation and risk-taking, then you might look for candidates who have a track record of trying new things and taking calculated risks.

2. **Develop interview questions**: Once you have defined the company culture, develop interview questions that will help you assess whether a candidate is a good cultural fit. For example, you might ask questions such as:

- Can you tell me about a time when you had to take a risk in your work?
- How did you approach it?
- How do you work with others in a team? Can you describe a project where you collaborated with others to achieve a goal?
- How do you handle failure or setbacks in your work?

3. **Look for shared values**: During the interview process, pay attention to whether the candidate shares the company's values. For example, if your startup values teamwork and collaboration, you might look for candidates who demonstrate that they work well with others and value cooperation. You might also look for candidates who have a passion for the company's mission or industry.

4. **Consider the working environment**: A candidate's cultural fit also depends on whether they will thrive in your startup's working environment. For example, if your startup has a fast-paced, high-pressure work environment, you might look for candidates who have experience working in similar environments and can handle stress well.

5. **Check references**: Finally, check the candidate's references to get a sense of how they have worked in other environments. Ask the references about the candidate's work style, their ability to collaborate with others, and

how they handle challenges.

Example:

Let's say you are hiring for a startup that values innovation and creativity. Here are some interview questions and evaluation criteria you might use to assess a candidate's cultural fit:

Interview Questions:

-Can you tell me about a project where you had to think outside the box and come up with a creative solution?

-How do you stay up to date with industry trends and new technologies?

-How do you approach problem-solving in your work?

Evaluation Criteria:

-Does the candidate have a track record of creative thinking and innovation?

-Do they show a passion for the industry and an eagerness to learn?

-Do they approach problem-solving in a way that aligns with the company's values?

Hire for potential:

Hiring for potential is an essential strategy for startups. It involves looking beyond a candidate's current skills and experience and assessing their ability to learn, adapt, and grow with the company. Here are some detailed steps and examples for hiring for potential in a startup:

1. **Identify the key skills and traits required for the role:** Before you begin the hiring process, it's essential to define the skills and traits that are necessary for the role. Consider the specific needs of your startup and the culture you're trying to build. For example, if you're looking for a salesperson, you might prioritize skills such as communication, negotiation, and resilience.

2. **Look for a growth mindset:** When evaluating potential hires, look for those who have a growth mindset. This means they believe their abilities can be developed through dedication and hard work, rather than being fixed traits. They are open to learning and trying new things, even if they fail. For example, a candidate who has taken on challenging projects or pursued additional education on their own demonstrates a growth mindset.

3. **Assess their ability to learn quickly:** Startups move quickly, and you need employees who can keep up. Look for candidates who have a track record of learning quickly and applying new information. For example, a

candidate who has worked in a variety of roles or industries and adapted to each new challenge shows they can learn quickly.

4. **Consider their passion for your industry:** Passion is a critical component of potential. Look for candidates who are genuinely excited about your industry and what your startup is trying to achieve. They are more likely to be motivated to learn and grow within your company. For example, a candidate who has volunteered or worked in a related field demonstrates passion for the industry.

5. **Evaluate their problem-solving skills:** Startups often face unexpected challenges, and you need employees who can think on their feet and solve problems quickly. Look for candidates who have a history of taking initiative to solve problems. For example, a candidate who has implemented new systems or processes to streamline operations demonstrates strong problem-solving skills.

6. **Conduct behavioral interviews:** Behavioral interviews are an effective way to assess a candidate's potential. These interviews focus on the candidate's past experiences and behaviors to predict future performance. Ask open-ended questions that require the candidate to describe specific situations and how they handled them. For example, you might ask, "Tell me about a time when you had to learn a new skill quickly. How did you go about it?"

7. **Provide growth opportunities:** Once you've hired a candidate with potential, it's essential to provide opportunities for growth and development. Offer training, mentorship, and new challenges to help them develop their skills and reach their potential within your company. For example, you might assign a new hire to work on a project with a senior employee to provide mentorship and guidance.

In summary, hiring for potential involves looking beyond a candidate's current skills and experience and assessing their ability to learn, adapt, and grow with your startup. Look for candidates with a growth mindset, a passion for your industry, strong problem-solving skills, and a track record of learning quickly. Use behavioral interviews to assess potential and provide growth opportunities to help your new hires reach their potential within your company.

How to motivate anyone to join your startup?

Motivating someone to join a startup at an early stage can be challenging since there are many unknowns and risks involved. However, here are some tips that may help:

1. **Share your vision**: Start by sharing your vision and the mission of the startup. Explain why you started the company, what problem you are trying to solve, and how you plan to do it. Make sure to communicate your passion and excitement for the project.

2. **Emphasize the impact**: Highlight the potential impact that the startup can have on the world, the industry, or the market. Explain how joining the team can be a unique opportunity to contribute to something meaningful and make a real difference.

3. **Offer equity**: Equity is a powerful motivator for people who are willing to take a risk and join an early-stage startup. Offer a fair and competitive equity package that aligns with the person's role and responsibilities.

4. **Emphasize the learning opportunity**: Joining an early-stage startup can be a great learning experience. Highlight the potential to learn new skills, take on new challenges, and work with talented and passionate people.

5. **Create a strong team culture**: Emphasize the importance of building a strong team culture and creating a supportive and collaborative work environment. Highlight the opportunities for professional and personal growth that come with being part of a startup.

6. **Be transparent**: Be honest and transparent about the risks and challenges involved in joining an early-stage startup. Make sure to communicate the potential risks and challenges upfront so that candidates can make an informed decision.

Overall, motivating someone to join an early-stage startup requires a combination of passion, vision, and transparency. By highlighting the potential impact, learning opportunity, and equity package, you can attract talented individuals who are willing to take a risk and join your team.

Importance of a Co-Founder

The analogy of "marrying" a co-founder for a startup is often used because starting a business with a co-founder requires a similar level of commitment, communication, and trust as a marriage.

Just like a marriage, starting a business with a co-founder is a long-term commitment that requires a significant investment of time, energy, and resources. It is important to choose a co-founder who shares your values, vision, and work ethic, and who you can trust to make decisions that are in the best interest of the business.

Similarly to a marriage, there may be disagreements, conflicts, and difficult times along the way, but a strong and healthy relationship between co-founders can help to navigate these challenges and ensure the success of the business.

Finally, just as a marriage requires open and effective communication, starting a business with a co-founder requires regular and honest communication to ensure that both parties are on the same page and working towards the same goals.

Hence, the analogy of "marrying" a co-founder for a startup emphasizes the importance of choosing the right partner for a long-term commitment and building a strong and healthy relationship to ensure the success of the business.

Having a co-founder for a startup can provide numerous benefits, some of which include:

- **Shared workload:** Starting a business is a daunting task that requires a lot of work. Having a co-founder allows you to share the workload and responsibilities, allowing each of you to focus on your strengths and expertise. This can also help to reduce stress and burnout.

- **Complementary skills:** A co-founder with complementary skills can help to fill gaps in your own skillset. For example, if you are a technical person, having a co-founder with a strong business background can help to balance your skills and improve the overall success of the business.

- **Increased motivation:** Starting a business can be a lonely journey. Having a co-founder can provide you with someone to bounce ideas off, share the highs and lows of the journey, and provide moral support. This can help to keep you motivated and focused on achieving your goals.

- **Access to resources:** A co-founder can bring their own network of contacts and resources to the business. This can include access to investors, industry experts, or potential customers. This can help to accelerate the growth of the business and improve its chances of success.

- **Better decision-making:** Having a co-founder can provide a sounding board for important decisions. This can help to ensure that decisions are made with careful consideration and multiple perspectives are taken into account.

How to find a right co-founder?

Identifying the right co-founder for your startup can be a challenging and critical task. Here are some steps to help you identify the right co-founder for your startup:

1. **Determine the Skills You Need**: Before you start looking for a co-founder, you should identify the skills that are essential for your startup. Make a list of the skills required for your business, such as technical, marketing, or business development. This will help you to identify the right co-founder who can complement your skills and bring expertise in areas where you might be lacking.

2. **Look for Someone Who Shares Your Vision**: Finding a co-founder who shares your vision and values is essential. Look for someone who is passionate about your idea and has a clear understanding of your business objectives. This person should be able to work with you to achieve your goals and be committed to the success of the startup.

3. **Evaluate Their Experience:** Evaluate the experience of your potential co-founder. Look for someone who has relevant experience in your industry or a similar industry. This experience will help them to contribute meaningfully to your startup and make informed decisions.

4. **Check Their Compatibility:** Compatibility is essential for a successful partnership. Look for someone who you can work with effectively and have a good rapport. This person should be able to communicate effectively and resolve conflicts amicably.

5. **Test Their Commitment:** Look for a co-founder who is willing to commit to your startup for the long-term. This person should be willing to put in the time and effort required to make your startup a success. Test their commitment by asking them about their past experiences and how they have handled challenging situations.

6. **Conduct Background Checks:** Before you bring on a co-founder, conduct a thorough background check. Look for any red flags, such as a history of litigation or bankruptcy, that could indicate potential issues down the line.

Examples:

- Airbnb: Brian Chesky and Joe Gebbia met at the Rhode Island School of Design, where they both studied design. They shared a vision for creating a platform that would enable people to rent out their homes to travelers. Chesky brought technical expertise, while Gebbia brought design skills to the partnership.

- Apple: Steve Jobs and Steve Wozniak met in the 1970s and bonded over their love of electronics. Jobs brought marketing and design skills to the partnership, while Wozniak brought technical expertise. Together, they created some of the most iconic products of our time.

- Google: Larry Page and Sergey Brin met at Stanford University, where they were both studying computer science. They bonded over their love of technology and a shared vision for organizing the world's information. Page brought business acumen, while Brin brought technical expertise to the partnership.

In summary, having a co-founder for a startup can bring many benefits, including shared workload, complementary skills, increased motivation, access to resources, and better decision-making. However, it is important to choose the right co-founder and establish clear communication and expectations to ensure a successful partnership.

CHAPTER NINE

Organic ways to market

Organic marketing is a cost-effective and sustainable way for startups to promote their products or services without spending a lot of money on advertising. It involves using free or low-cost marketing techniques to reach potential customers through various online and offline channels. In this chapter, we will discuss some of the most effective organic marketing strategies for startups and provide examples to help illustrate how they work.

Define your target audience

As discussed in the previous chapters,

Defining the target audience for organic marketing of a startup is an important step in creating an effective marketing strategy. It involves identifying the group of people who are most likely to be interested in your product or service and tailoring your marketing efforts to meet their needs and preferences. Here are the steps to define the target audience for organic marketing of a startup in detail with examples:

1. Conduct Market Research: Conduct market research to identify the demographics, interests, and behavior of your potential customers. This can be done through online surveys, focus groups, or by using tools like Google Analytics.

Example: If your startup is a vegan meal delivery service, you might conduct market research to identify the demographics of people who are interested in plant-based diets, their income level, and their location.

2. Define Demographics: Once you have conducted market research, define the demographics of your target audience. This includes their age, gender, education, income, and location.

Example: The target audience for the vegan meal delivery service might be women between the ages of 25-45 who live in urban areas, have a higher education level, and earn above-average income.

3. Identify Psychographics: Psychographics refers to the interests, values, and lifestyles of your target audience. This information can be gathered from social media profiles or through online surveys.

Example: The target audience for the vegan meal delivery service might be health-conscious individuals who value sustainability and ethical eating practices.

4. Analyze Competitors: Analyze the marketing strategies of your competitors to identify the gaps in the market that your startup can fill. This can help you to differentiate your product or service and target a specific group of customers.

Example: If there are other vegan meal delivery services in the market, analyze their marketing strategies to identify gaps in the market. Perhaps they do not offer gluten-free options, or their delivery times are too long.

5. Develop Personas: Based on the information gathered from market research and competitor analysis, develop buyer personas. These are fictional representations of your ideal customer and can be used to tailor your marketing messages to meet their needs.

Example: The vegan meal delivery service might develop a buyer persona named "Sustainable Sarah," a health-conscious woman in her 30s who is interested in reducing her environmental footprint and values ethical eating practices.

Content Marketing

Building a content marketing strategy for organic marketing can help your startup increase brand awareness, generate leads, and ultimately drive conversions. Here are the steps you can take to create an effective content marketing strategy for your startup:

-**Define your target audience:** Before you start creating content, you need to know who your target audience is. What are their pain points, interests, and goals? This will help you create content that resonates with them and addresses their needs.

Example: If you are a startup that offers a project management tool for small businesses, your target audience could be entrepreneurs, small business owners, or project managers who are looking for an affordable and easy-to-use solution to manage their projects.

-Identify your content goals: What do you want your content to achieve? Are you trying to increase brand awareness, generate leads, or drive conversions? Identifying your content goals will help you create content that aligns with your overall business objectives.

Example: If your goal is to generate leads, you may want to create content that educates your audience about project management best practices and positions your tool as the solution.

-**Conduct a content audit:** Before you start creating new content, take a look at what you already have. Identify the content that has performed well in terms of engagement, shares, and conversions. This will help you understand what type of content resonates with your audience and what gaps you need to fill.

Example: If you find that your blog posts on project management tips and tricks have generated a lot of engagement, you may want to create more of that type of content.

-**Develop a content calendar:** A content calendar will help you plan and organize your content for the coming weeks or months. It should include the topics you will cover, the type of content you will create (e.g., blog posts, videos, infographics), and the publishing schedule.

Example: If you decide to create a blog post on project management tips every week, your content calendar could include the topics you will cover for the next few months, the publishing date, and the writer responsible for each post.

-**Create content:** Based on your content goals, target audience, and content audit, start creating content that addresses your audience's needs and interests. Make sure your content is high-quality, informative, and relevant to your audience.

Example: You could create blog posts on project management tips, how-to videos on using your tool, and infographics on project management statistics.

-**Promote your content:** Creating great content is just the first step. You also need to promote it to ensure it reaches your target audience. Promote your content on social media, through email marketing, and by reaching out to influencers and other relevant websites.

Example: You could promote your blog posts on project management tips on social media by sharing them on your company's LinkedIn, Facebook, and Twitter pages. You could also reach out to influencers in the project management space and ask them to share your content with their followers.

-**Analyze and optimize:** Finally, track your content performance and make changes as needed. Use analytics tools to measure engagement, shares, and conversions, and adjust your content strategy accordingly.

Example: If you find that your videos on using your project management tool are not generating as many views as you would like, you may want to try a different format, such as a webinar or live demo.

In summary, creating a content marketing strategy for organic marketing requires a deep understanding of your target audience, clear content goals, and a well-planned content calendar. By creating high-quality content that resonates with your audience and promoting it effectively, you can increase brand awareness, generate leads, and drive conversions for your startup.

Search Engine Optimization (SEO)

SEO (Search Engine Optimization) is the process of optimizing a website or online content to improve its visibility and ranking in search engine results pages (SERPs). Implementing SEO strategies can help startups increase their online presence and attract more organic traffic to their website. Here are some SEO strategies and examples for organic marketing of a startup:

- **Keyword Research:** Keyword research is the process of identifying and analyzing the search terms that potential customers use when searching for products or services online. Startups can use keyword research tools like Google Keyword Planner, Ahrefs, SEMRush, or Moz to identify relevant keywords for their business.

For example, if a startup sells handmade soaps, relevant keywords might include "handmade soap," "organic soap," "natural soap," "best soap for sensitive skin," etc. Once you have identified the relevant keywords, use them in your website content, meta tags, titles, descriptions, etc.

- **On-Page Optimization:** On-page optimization involves optimizing your website's pages for search engines and users. This includes optimizing your website's content, titles, descriptions, headings, images, and URLs.

For example, a startup selling handmade soaps could optimize their product pages by including relevant keywords in the page titles, descriptions, and headings, as well as adding high-quality product images and informative product descriptions.

- **Content Marketing:** Content marketing involves creating and sharing valuable, relevant, and consistent content to attract and retain a clearly defined audience. Content marketing can help startups build brand awareness, generate leads, and improve their search engine rankings.

For example, a startup selling handmade soaps could create a blog that features articles on topics related to soap-making, such as "The Benefits of Using Natural Soap" or "DIY Soap-Making Tips." These blog posts could be optimized with relevant keywords and shared on social media to attract more visitors to the website.

- **Link Building:** Link building involves acquiring links from other websites to your website. Search engines view backlinks as a vote of confidence in the quality of your website's content.

For example, a startup selling handmade soaps could reach out to beauty bloggers and ask them to review their products and link back to their website. They could also participate in online forums and communities related to soap-making and share their expertise while including a link back to their website.

- **Local SEO:** Local SEO involves optimizing your website for local search queries. This is particularly important for startups that rely on local customers to drive sales.

For example, a startup selling handmade soaps in a specific location could optimize their website for local search queries by including their address and phone number on their website, creating a Google My Business listing, and using location-specific keywords in their content.

Overall, implementing these SEO strategies can help startups increase their visibility in search engine results pages, attract more organic traffic to their website, and ultimately drive more sales.

Social Media Marketing

Social media marketing can be a powerful tool for startups to reach their target audience and build brand awareness. Here are some strategies to increase organic reach on social media:

1. Define your target audience: Before you start creating content, you need to define your target audience. This will help you tailor your messaging and content to reach the people who are most likely to engage with your brand.

2. Choose the right platforms: Not all social media platforms are created equal, and different platforms have different audiences. Choose the platforms that your target audience is most likely to use and focus your efforts there.

3. Create engaging content: Social media users are bombarded with content every day, so it's important to create content that stands out. Use eye-catching visuals, write compelling captions, and include calls-to-action to encourage engagement.

4. Use hashtags: Hashtags can help your content get discovered by users who are searching for specific topics. Research relevant hashtags and include them in your posts.

5. Engage with your audience: Social media is a two-way conversation. Respond to comments and messages, and engage with your followers by liking and sharing their content.

6. Collaborate with influencers: Influencers have large followings and can help you reach a wider audience. Find influencers who align with your brand and work with them to create content that promotes your products or services.

7. Run contests and giveaways: Contests and giveaways can help increase engagement and generate buzz around your brand. Encourage users to share your content and follow your social media accounts for a chance to win a prize.

Examples:

Let's say you're a startup that sells eco-friendly beauty products. Your target audience is environmentally-conscious women between the ages of 18 and 35. Here are some examples of social media marketing strategies you could use:

- Instagram: Instagram is a great platform for visual content. Create visually-appealing images and videos that showcase your products and their eco-friendly features. Use relevant hashtags like #greenbeauty and #ecofriendlybeauty to reach a wider audience. Collaborate with influencers in the beauty industry who share your values.

- Facebook: Facebook is a great platform for building a community around your brand. Create a Facebook group for your customers where they can ask questions, share tips, and connect with each other. Share blog posts and articles about eco-friendly living to provide value to your audience.

- TikTok: TikTok is a platform that has exploded in popularity in recent years. Create short videos that showcase your products and their benefits in a fun and engaging way. Use trending hashtags like #sustainableliving and #greenbeauty to reach a wider audience.

- Twitter: Twitter is a platform that moves fast, so it's important to keep up with the latest trends and news. Use Twitter to share industry news and tips for eco-friendly living. Run Twitter polls to engage your audience and get feedback on your products.

- LinkedIn: LinkedIn is a great platform for B2B marketing. Use LinkedIn to showcase your company's mission and values, and share content that positions your brand as a thought leader in the eco-friendly beauty industry. Connect with other businesses and individuals who share your values and collaborate on content.

- YouTube: YouTube is a great platform for long-form video content. Create tutorial videos that showcase how to use your products, or interview industry experts about eco-friendly living. Use keywords and tags to optimize your videos for search.

Public Relations:

Public relations (PR) can be a powerful tool for organic marketing for startups. PR focuses on building and maintaining relationships between the startup and its public, including customers, investors, and media outlets. By using PR, startups can increase brand awareness, generate buzz, and attract new customers without spending a lot of money on traditional advertising.

Here are some ways in which PR can help startups with their organic marketing efforts:

1. **Press releases:** One of the most common ways PR can help startups is through press releases. Press releases can be used to announce new products, services, or events, or to share news about the startup, such as fundraising or new hires. These releases can be distributed to various media outlets, which can result in coverage and exposure for the startup.

Example: A startup that creates an innovative fitness tracking app can issue a press release to announce a new feature that tracks sleep patterns.

This press release can be picked up by fitness and wellness publications, resulting in increased exposure for the startup.

2. Thought leadership: PR can also help startups establish themselves as thought leaders in their industry. By positioning founders or key executives as experts, startups can gain credibility and authority, which can help attract customers and investors.

Example: A startup that provides virtual event planning services can have its founder write an article about the future of virtual events for a business publication. This article can position the founder as an expert in the field, leading to increased exposure and potentially attracting new customers.

3. Social media: PR can also be used to increase a startup's presence on social media. By creating and sharing engaging content, startups can attract followers and build relationships with their audience.

Example: A startup that creates a sustainable fashion line can use social media to share behind-the-scenes content, showcase its products, and share information about the company's sustainability initiatives. This can help the startup attract a following of environmentally conscious consumers.

4. Influencer partnerships: PR can also help startups build partnerships with influencers in their industry. These partnerships can help increase brand awareness and attract new customers.

Example: A startup that creates a healthy meal delivery service can partner with fitness influencers to showcase its meals and promote its service to their followers. This can help the startup attract a new audience of health-conscious consumers.

In conclusion, public relations can be an effective tool for startups looking to increase brand awareness, generate buzz, and attract new customers. By using press releases, thought leadership, social media, and influencer partnerships, startups can leverage PR to achieve their organic marketing goals.

Email Marketing:

Email marketing is a powerful tool for organic marketing for startups. It involves sending promotional emails to a list of subscribers who have shown interest in your business. These subscribers can be acquired through various channels like social media, landing pages, events, or by offering incentives for signing up.

Here are some ways email marketing can help with organic marketing for startups:

- **Building relationships with customers**: Email marketing helps you build a personal relationship with your subscribers by providing them with useful and relevant content. You can use email campaigns to educate them about your product, share industry news and insights, and offer exclusive discounts and promotions.

Example: A startup that sells organic skincare products can send emails to its subscribers with tips on how to maintain healthy skin, information about the benefits of using natural ingredients, and exclusive offers on its products.

- **Driving traffic to your website**: You can use email marketing to drive traffic to your website by including links to your blog posts, product pages, and landing pages in your emails. This can help increase your website's visibility and improve your search engine rankings.

Example: A startup that sells online courses on digital marketing can send emails to its subscribers with links to its blog posts on the latest digital marketing trends and tips, and encourage them to sign up for its courses.

- **Boosting brand awareness**: Email marketing can help you increase brand awareness by reminding your subscribers about your brand and what it stands for. You can use email campaigns to promote your brand values, mission, and vision.

Example: A startup that offers sustainable fashion products can send emails to its subscribers with information about the benefits of sustainable fashion and its impact on the environment.

- **Generating leads and sales**: Email marketing is an effective way to generate leads and sales for your startup. You can use email campaigns to promote your products, offer exclusive discounts and promotions, and encourage your subscribers to make a purchase.

Example: A startup that sells organic food products can send emails to its subscribers with information about its latest products, recipes using its products, and exclusive discounts on its products.

In conclusion, email marketing is an essential tool for organic marketing for startups. It can help you build relationships with customers, drive traffic to your website, boost brand awareness, and generate leads and sales. By providing your subscribers with valuable and relevant content, you can establish yourself as a thought leader in your industry and build a loyal customer base.

Host events:

Hosting or attending events can be a great way to market a startup organically. Here are some ways to make the most of events:

1. **Host your own event:** Hosting your own event can be a great way to showcase your startup and connect with potential customers, investors, and partners. For example, if you have a food-related startup, you could host a food festival or tasting event to showcase your products.

2. **Attend industry events:** Attending industry events can be a great way to network with potential customers and partners. For example, if you have a tech startup, you could attend tech conferences or hackathons to connect with other professionals in your industry.

3. **Collaborate with other startups**: Collaborating with other startups can help you reach a wider audience and create valuable partnerships. For example, you could co-host an event with another startup that targets a similar audience.

4. **Participate in community events:** Participating in community events can help you connect with potential customers and build goodwill in your local community. For example, you could sponsor a local charity event or participate in a community festival.

5. **Use social media to promote events:** Use social media to promote your events and encourage attendance. You could create an event page on Facebook or LinkedIn, use hashtags to promote the event on Twitter or Instagram, or create a short video to promote the event on YouTube.

Overall, events can be a great way to market your startup organically. By hosting your own events, attending industry events, collaborating with other startups, participating in community events, and using social media to promote events, you can reach a wider audience and build valuable connections with potential customers, investors, and partners.

Focus on customer experience

Testimonials and feedbacks can be powerful tools in the organic marketing of a startup. Here are some ways in which they can play a big role:

1. **Build trust:** Testimonials and feedbacks from satisfied customers can help build trust with potential customers. People are more likely to trust the opinions of others who have used your product or service than they are to

trust your own marketing messages.

2. **Increase credibility**: Testimonials and feedbacks can increase the credibility of your startup by providing social proof. When people see that others have had positive experiences with your product or service, they are more likely to believe that your startup is legitimate and trustworthy.

3. **Provide valuable insights**: Feedback from customers can provide valuable insights into what is working well and what needs improvement in your startup. This feedback can help you refine your product or service, and make changes that will better meet the needs of your customers.

4. **Create marketing content**: Testimonials and feedbacks can be used to create marketing content that can be shared across various channels. For example, you could create a video featuring satisfied customers sharing their experiences with your startup, or create a blog post highlighting positive reviews from customers.

5. **Increase customer loyalty**: When customers feel that their feedback is valued and acted upon, they are more likely to become loyal customers. By incorporating customer feedback into your product development and marketing strategies, you can create a culture of customer loyalty and advocacy.

Examples of startups that have successfully used testimonials and feedbacks include Airbnb, which prominently features guest reviews on their platform, and Slack, which has a dedicated customer feedback channel to gather insights and suggestions from users. By leveraging the power of testimonials and feedbacks, startups can build trust, increase credibility, gain valuable insights, create marketing content, and increase customer loyalty.

By using a combination of content marketing, SEO, social media marketing, PR, and email marketing, startups can attract potential customers, build brand awareness, and establish themselves as industry leaders.

Here comes the bonus!

Facebook Marketing

Marketing on Facebook organically can be a great way for startups to promote their brand, reach new customers, and build a community around their product or service. Here are some steps to consider when creating a

Facebook marketing strategy for your startup:

- **Define your target audience**: Before you start promoting your brand on Facebook, it's important to know who your target audience is. Consider factors like age, gender, location, interests, and behaviors to help you create content that will resonate with your audience.

Example: If you're a startup that sells eco-friendly products, your target audience may be environmentally-conscious consumers who are interested in sustainable living and reducing their carbon footprint.

- **Create a Facebook Page:** Once you know your target audience, create a Facebook Page for your startup. Make sure to include a clear and concise description of your brand, along with your contact information and links to your website and other social media accounts.

Example: If you're a startup that sells eco-friendly products, your Facebook Page should include information about your brand's mission, the types of products you sell, and how your products can help people live a more sustainable lifestyle.

- **Post engaging content:** To keep your followers engaged and interested in your brand, post a variety of content on your Facebook Page. This can include images, videos, blog posts, infographics, and more. Make sure your content is informative, entertaining, and relevant to your audience.

Example: If you're a startup that sells eco-friendly products, you could create a blog post about the benefits of using natural cleaning products, share an infographic about the environmental impact of plastic waste, or post a video showing how to use your products in everyday life.

- **Use Facebook Groups:** Join relevant Facebook Groups where your target audience is likely to be active. Participate in discussions, offer helpful advice, and share your brand's content when appropriate. This can help you build relationships with potential customers and establish yourself as an authority in your industry.

Example: If you're a startup that sells eco-friendly products, you could join Facebook Groups for environmental activists, zero-waste enthusiasts, or sustainable living communities.

- **Run Contests and Giveaways:** Running contests and giveaways on Facebook can help you attract new followers and engage your existing audience. Make sure to follow Facebook's guidelines for running contests and promotions.

Example: If you're a startup that sells eco-friendly products, you could run a contest asking followers to share a photo of how they use your products to live a more sustainable lifestyle. The winner could receive a free product or a discount on their next purchase.

- **Collaborate with Influencers:** Partnering with influencers who have a large following in your target audience can help you reach new customers and increase your brand's visibility. Look for influencers who share your brand's values and are a good fit for your product or service.

Example: If you're a startup that sells eco-friendly products, you could partner with an influencer who is passionate about sustainability and shares your commitment to reducing waste.

- **Analyze Your Results:** Finally, it's important to track and analyze your Facebook marketing efforts to see what's working and what's not. Use Facebook Insights to monitor your Page's performance and make adjustments as needed.

Example: If you're a startup that sells eco-friendly products, you could track metrics like engagement rate, reach, and website clicks to see which types of content are resonating with your audience and driving the most traffic to your website.

Instagram marketing

Instagram has become one of the most popular social media platforms with over a billion active users. It is a great platform for startups to market their products or services organically. Here are some steps you can take to create an effective organic Instagram marketing strategy for your startup:

- **Define your target audience:** Identify the audience you want to reach, and tailor your content to meet their needs and interests.

- **Create a content strategy:** Develop a content strategy that aligns with your target audience's interests and needs. It should be a mix of product or service-focused content, behind-the-scenes content, and user-generated content.

- **Optimize your profile:** Make sure your Instagram profile is optimized to attract your target audience. Use a recognizable profile picture, write a compelling bio, and include a link to your website.

- **Use hashtags:** Hashtags are a great way to reach new audiences on Instagram. Use relevant hashtags in your posts and stories to increase your visibility.

- **Engage with your audience**: Engage with your followers by responding to comments and direct messages. It will help to build a loyal following and establish trust.

- **Collaborate with influencers:** Identify influencers in your industry and collaborate with them to promote your product or service. They can help to increase your visibility and reach new audiences.

- **Use Instagram stories:** Instagram stories are a great way to engage with your audience and share behind-the-scenes content. Use features like polls and questions to encourage engagement.

- **Measure your results:** Measure your Instagram marketing results to understand what works and what doesn't. Use analytics tools to track your engagement rate, reach, and follower growth.

Here are some examples of startups that have successfully used Instagram for organic marketing:

- Glossier: Glossier has built a loyal following on Instagram by using user-generated content and behind-the-scenes content. They also use hashtags like #glossierpink to create a recognizable brand image.

- Hims: Hims uses Instagram to share educational content about their products and services. They also collaborate with influencers to reach new audiences and build trust.

- Rothy's: Rothy's uses Instagram to showcase their sustainable and eco-friendly products. They also use Instagram stories to share behind-the-scenes content and engage with their followers.

Overall, the key to a successful organic Instagram marketing strategy for your startup is to create content that resonates with your target audience and engages them in a meaningful way. By following these steps and learning from successful examples, you can build a strong presence on Instagram and grow your business.

LinkedIn marketing

LinkedIn is a powerful platform for marketing your startup, especially if you're targeting professionals and businesses. Here are some organic ways to market your startup on LinkedIn:

- **Define your target audience:** Determine who your ideal customers are and what they need from your product or service. Look at LinkedIn groups and communities where your potential customers may be active.

- **Optimize your LinkedIn profile:** Ensure that your profile is complete and up-to-date with a professional profile picture, a headline that describes what you do, and a summary that showcases your startup's value proposition. Include relevant keywords in your profile to improve your search rankings.

- **Create valuable content:** Produce content that your target audience will find useful and informative. Share articles, infographics, or videos that demonstrate your expertise and solve your customer's pain points. Consider starting a blog on your website and sharing your articles on LinkedIn.

- **Engage with your audience:** Engage with your followers by responding to comments and messages promptly. Share posts from other thought leaders in your industry, like and comment on posts in your feed. Participate in relevant LinkedIn groups and communities to join conversations and contribute to the discussion.

- **Leverage LinkedIn's features:** Utilize LinkedIn features like LinkedIn Live, LinkedIn Stories, and LinkedIn Polls to engage your audience and showcase your brand.

- **Connect with influencers:** Identify influencers in your industry and connect with them on LinkedIn. Engage with their content, and consider collaborating with them on content or projects to expand your reach.

- **Measure your success:** Use LinkedIn Analytics to track your engagement and see which content is resonating with your audience. Adjust your strategy based on what's working.

Examples of organic LinkedIn marketing for startups:

- Post thought leadership content: For example, a SaaS startup could publish a blog post on their website about how to use their product to improve productivity. They could then share this post on LinkedIn and tag relevant industry leaders to get their attention.

- Share company culture: A startup could share a photo of their team at a company event or working remotely, showcasing their brand's personality and values.

- Leverage LinkedIn groups: A startup in the healthcare industry could join relevant LinkedIn groups and engage with members by sharing useful information about their products.

- Create a LinkedIn poll: A startup could create a poll asking their followers which feature they would like to see added to their product next. This is a great way to engage with your audience and get valuable feedback.

- Collaborate with influencers: A fintech startup could partner with a well-known personal finance influencer to create a LinkedIn Live event where they discuss budgeting tips and showcase how the startup's product can help viewers save money.

In conclusion, organic marketing can be a powerful way for startups to promote their products or services without breaking the bank.

CHAPTER TEN

Inorganic ways to market

Inorganic marketing methods refer to paid or non-organic ways of promoting a startup or business. Inorganic methods of marketing can be effective for startups looking to build awareness, generate leads, and increase their customer base quickly. Here are some examples of inorganic marketing methods that startups can use:

Pay-per-click (PPC) advertising

Pay-per-click (PPC) advertising is a digital advertising model where advertisers pay each time a user clicks on one of their ads. In this model, advertisers bid on keywords that are relevant to their target audience and create ads that will appear in search engine results or on websites that are part of an advertising network. When a user clicks on an ad, the advertiser is charged a fee, which is based on the bidding price for the particular keyword or placement.

PPC advertising can be a powerful way to drive traffic to a website or promote a product or service. It is particularly effective for businesses that want to reach a specific audience with a high level of intent, as users who click on PPC ads are often actively searching for a particular product or service.

Here are some examples of PPC advertising:

- Google Ads: Google Ads is the largest PPC advertising platform, and it allows businesses to create ads that will appear in search engine results pages (SERPs) or on websites that are part of the Google Display Network. Advertisers bid on keywords that are relevant to their business, and Google uses a complex algorithm to determine which ads will be shown and in what order.

- Facebook Ads: Facebook Ads allows businesses to create ads that will appear on the Facebook platform, including in users' newsfeeds or on the right-hand side of the screen. Advertisers can target their ads based on a range of demographic and behavioral factors, such as age, location, interests, and past online behavior.

- Amazon Ads: Amazon Ads is a PPC advertising platform that allows businesses to promote their products on the Amazon website. Advertisers bid on keywords that are relevant to their products, and their ads will appear in search results or on product detail pages.

- Bing Ads: Bing Ads is a PPC advertising platform that operates similarly to Google Ads, but with a smaller audience. Advertisers can create ads that will appear in Bing search results or on websites that are part of the Bing Network.

PPC advertising can be a cost-effective way to reach a targeted audience and drive conversions. However, it requires careful planning and optimization to ensure that campaigns are effective and profitable. Advertisers must continually monitor their campaigns, test different ad copy and targeting options, and adjust their bids to achieve the best possible results.

Social media advertising:

Social media advertising is a powerful tool for promoting a startup and reaching a wider audience. Inorganic marketing refers to paid advertising, where businesses pay for their content to be promoted on social media platforms. In this answer, I will explain social media advertising for inorganic marketing for a startup in detail with examples.

1. **Identify the target audience:** The first step in social media advertising is to identify the target audience. The target audience for a startup may be people who are interested in the product or service being offered, people within a specific age group or location, or people with a specific interest. For example, a startup that sells eco-friendly products may target people who are interested in sustainability.

2. **Choose the right social media platform:** Once the target audience has been identified, the next step is to choose the right social media platform

to advertise on. Different social media platforms have different audiences and advertising options. For example, if the target audience is young adults, advertising on Instagram may be more effective than advertising on Facebook.

3. **Set a budget**: Social media advertising can be expensive, so it's important to set a budget. The budget should be based on the goals of the advertising campaign, the target audience, and the cost of advertising on the chosen social media platform.

4. **Create engaging content**: The content of the advertisement should be engaging and appealing to the target audience. The content should include images, videos, and/or text that highlight the benefits of the product or service being offered. For example, a startup that sells vegan food products may create an advertisement with images of delicious vegan dishes and text that highlights the health benefits of a plant-based diet.

5. **Use targeted advertising**: Social media platforms offer targeted advertising options that allow businesses to reach a specific audience. For example, Facebook allows businesses to target their advertisements based on demographics, interests, behaviors, and more.

6. **Monitor and analyze results**: It's important to monitor the results of social media advertising campaigns and analyze the data to make improvements. Social media platforms offer analytics tools that allow businesses to track the performance of their advertisements. Based on the data, adjustments can be made to the advertising campaign to improve its effectiveness.

Example:

Let's say there is a startup that sells handmade jewelry. The target audience is women aged 25-40 who are interested in fashion and accessories. The startup decides to advertise on Instagram as it is a platform that has a large audience of women interested in fashion.

The startup sets a budget of $500 for the advertising campaign. They create engaging content for the advertisement, including images of their jewelry and text that highlights the unique handmade aspect of their products.

They use targeted advertising on Instagram to reach their target audience. They select demographics that match their target audience and interests related to fashion and accessories.

After the advertising campaign is launched, they monitor the results using Instagram's analytics tools. They find that the advertisement has reached 10,000 people and has received 500 clicks to their website. Based on this data, they decide to make adjustments to the advertisement to improve its effectiveness. They decide to increase the budget of the campaign and add a call-to-action button to encourage more clicks to their website.

In conclusion, social media advertising is an effective way for startups to reach a wider audience and promote their products or services. By following the steps outlined above and using targeted advertising, startups can create engaging content and analyze the results of their campaigns to make improvements.

Influencer marketing

Influencer marketing is a type of marketing that involves collaborating with individuals who have a large following on social media to promote a product or service. Inorganic marketing refers to any type of marketing that is paid for, rather than earned through organic means such as search engine optimization or social media engagement.

For a startup, influencer marketing can be another powerful tool to reach a wider audience and generate brand awareness. Here are some steps to follow when implementing an influencer marketing campaign:

1. Define your target audience: The first step is to identify the audience you want to reach. Who are your potential customers and where do they spend their time online?

2. Research potential influencers: Look for influencers who have a following that matches your target audience. Look for influencers who are active on social media platforms where your audience is active.

3. Reach out to influencers: Once you have identified potential influencers, reach out to them to discuss a collaboration. Some influencers may require payment for their services, while others may be willing to work in exchange for free products or services.

4. Create a campaign: Work with the influencer to create a campaign that aligns with your brand and appeals to their audience. This can include sponsored posts, giveaways, or product reviews.

5. Track and measure results: Track the results of your influencer marketing campaign to determine its effectiveness. This can include metrics such as engagement, reach, and sales.

Here are a few examples of successful influencer marketing campaigns by startups:

- Glossier: Glossier is a beauty startup that has used influencer marketing to great effect. They work with a network of micro-influencers who share their products with their followers. This has helped them to create a strong brand identity and reach a wider audience.

- Casper: Casper is a mattress startup that has used influencer marketing to generate buzz around their products. They work with influencers in the home decor and lifestyle niches to showcase their mattresses in creative and engaging ways.

- HelloFresh: HelloFresh is a meal kit delivery service that has used influencer marketing to generate awareness and drive sales. They work with food bloggers and chefs to create recipes featuring their products, which helps to position them as a high-quality meal solution.

Overall, influencer marketing can be a powerful tool for startups to reach a wider audience and generate brand awareness. By identifying the right influencers and creating engaging campaigns, startups can effectively promote their products and services to potential customers.

Affiliate marketing

Affiliate marketing is a type of performance-based marketing in which a business rewards one or more affiliates for each customer brought about by the affiliate's marketing efforts. It is the process by which an affiliate earns a commission for marketing another person's or company's products. The affiliate simply searches for a product they enjoy, then promotes that product and earns a piece of the profit from each sale they make. It is a way for startups to get their products or services in front of a larger audience without spending a lot of money on advertising.

Here's how it works:

1. Identify potential affiliates: Start by identifying individuals or businesses that have an audience that is similar to your target market. These could be bloggers, influencers, content creators, or other startups.

2. Set up an affiliate program: Create an affiliate program that outlines the terms of the partnership. This should include the commission rate (i.e., the percentage of the sale that the affiliate will receive), how long the cookie duration (i.e., the amount of time between the click on the affiliate's link and the purchase) should be, and any other relevant details.

3. Provide marketing materials: Give your affiliates access to marketing materials such as banner ads, text links, and product images that they can use on their website or social media channels.

4. Monitor performance: Keep track of the traffic and sales that come from each affiliate to ensure that they are following the program rules and to calculate the commission owed.

5. Pay affiliates: Pay out commissions to your affiliates on a regular basis, such as monthly or quarterly.

Here are a few examples of startups that have successfully used affiliate marketing to grow their business:

- Dropbox: Dropbox is a cloud storage company that offers a referral program in which users can earn extra storage space by referring new users. For each referral, the user gets an additional 500MB of storage space, up to a maximum of 16GB. This program has helped Dropbox grow its user base from 100,000 to 4 million in just 15 months.

- Amazon: Amazon is one of the largest e-commerce retailers in the world and has a massive affiliate program with over a million affiliates. Amazon's affiliates earn a commission on every sale that comes from their referral link, and they can promote any product on Amazon's website.

- Bluehost: Bluehost is a web hosting company that offers a referral program for its customers. Affiliates earn a commission for every customer they refer to Bluehost who signs up for a hosting plan. This program has helped Bluehost become one of the largest web hosting companies in the world.

In summary, affiliate marketing can be an effective way for startups to reach a larger audience and generate more sales without spending a lot of money on advertising. By setting up an affiliate program, providing marketing materials, monitoring performance, and paying out commissions, startups can build relationships with affiliates and grow their business.

Trade shows and events

Trade shows and events are an effective form of inorganic marketing for startups. These events provide an opportunity for startups to showcase their products or services, interact with potential customers, and network with industry professionals. In this response, we'll dive into trade shows and events for startups in detail, including their benefits, how to prepare for them, and some examples of events that might be suitable for startups.

Benefits of Trade Shows and Events for Startups:

- **Increased brand exposure:** Trade shows and events are an opportunity to increase brand exposure for your startup. You can display your brand name and products or services to a large number of people in one place.
- **Networking opportunities:** Trade shows and events bring together a large number of industry professionals and potential customers. This provides an excellent opportunity for startups to network with potential partners, investors, and customers.

- **Customer interaction:** These events provide an opportunity for startups to interact with potential customers face-to-face. This interaction can be helpful in understanding customers' needs and feedback, and it can also help in building trust and brand loyalty.

- **Competitive analysis:** Trade shows and events are also an opportunity to analyze your competition. You can observe your competitors' products, marketing strategies, and customer interactions to improve your own approach.

Preparing for Trade Shows and Events:

- **Define your goals:** Determine what you hope to achieve from attending the event. Is it brand exposure, lead generation, or networking? Once you have defined your goals, you can tailor your approach to the event accordingly.

- **Prepare your pitch:** Prepare a concise and compelling pitch for your startup that will grab the attention of potential customers and investors.

- **Create marketing materials:** Develop marketing materials, such as brochures, business cards, and promotional items, that clearly convey your startup's products and services.

- **Train your team:** Ensure that your team is well-informed about your startup and its products or services. They should also be able to effectively communicate with potential customers and investors.

- **Make travel arrangements:** If the event is not in your city or region, make travel arrangements for your team and marketing materials.

Examples of Trade Shows and Events for Startups:

- CES: CES is a global technology event held annually in Las Vegas, Nevada. It showcases the latest in consumer electronics, software, and other technology products. Startups can exhibit their products, attend educational sessions, and network with industry professionals.

- SXSW: SXSW is an annual event held in Austin, Texas, that showcases interactive media, music, and film. Startups can showcase their products, participate in panel discussions, and network with industry professionals.

- Web Summit: Web Summit is a technology conference held annually in Lisbon, Portugal. It brings together startups, investors, and industry professionals to network and share ideas.

- TechCrunch Disrupt: TechCrunch Disrupt is an annual technology conference held in San Francisco, California. It brings together startups, investors, and industry professionals to showcase the latest in technology innovation and participate in panel discussions.

In conclusion, trade shows and events can be a highly effective form of inorganic marketing for startups. By carefully preparing and attending the right events, startups can increase brand exposure, network with industry professionals, interact with potential customers, and improve their competitive analysis. Examples of suitable events for startups include CES, SXSW, Web Summit, and TechCrunch Disrupt.

These are just a few examples of ways to market a startup inorganically. The key is to find the methods that work best for your business and target audience, and continually test and refine your approach to maximize your results.

Let's learn the inorganic ways!

Facebook Advertising

Running Facebook ads for a startup can be an effective way to drive traffic, increase brand awareness, and acquire customers. Here is a step-by-step guide on how to run Facebook ads for a startup, along with some examples:

1. Define Your Goals: Before running Facebook ads, it's essential to define your goals. Ask yourself, what do you want to achieve with your Facebook ads? Is it to increase brand awareness, generate leads, or drive sales? Having clear goals will help you create better ad campaigns.

Example: Suppose your startup is a new meal delivery service, and you want to generate leads to increase your customer base. Your goal would be to get people to sign up for your service.

2. Define Your Target Audience: Once you have defined your goals, the next step is to identify your target audience. Who are the people you want to reach with your Facebook ads? Consider demographics like age, gender, location, interests, and behaviors.

Example: For the meal delivery service startup, the target audience could be health-conscious individuals living in a specific location.

3. Create Your Ad Campaign: With your goals and target audience in mind, it's time to create your ad campaign. Facebook offers several ad formats, including image ads, video ads, carousel ads, and more.

Example: For the meal delivery service startup, you could create an image ad that showcases your healthy meals and highlights your sign-up offer.

4. Set Your Budget: Facebook ads work on a bidding system, which means you'll need to set a budget for your campaign. You can choose between a daily budget or a lifetime budget.

Example: If your startup has a small budget, you could start with a daily budget of $10 and increase it over time as you see results.

5. Monitor Your Ads: Once your ads are live, it's essential to monitor their performance regularly. Check your ad's metrics, including reach, engagement, and conversions, and make adjustments as needed.

Example: If your ad isn't generating enough leads, you could try targeting a different audience or adjusting your ad copy.

In conclusion, running Facebook ads for a startup involves defining your goals and target audience, creating your ad campaign, setting your budget, and monitoring your ads' performance. With the right strategy and approach, Facebook ads can be an effective way to grow your startup's customer base and increase brand awareness

Instagram Advertising

Here's the process and steps of running Instagram ads for a startup to follow:

Set up an Instagram Business Account: If you haven't already, create an Instagram Business account for your startup. This will give you access to Instagram Ads Manager, where you can create and manage your ads. To create an Instagram Business account, you need to have a Facebook page for your startup. Once you have a Facebook page, you can connect it to your Instagram account and switch to a Business account.

1. Define your target audience: Before you start creating your Instagram ad campaign, it's essential to define who your target audience is. Who are the people most likely to be interested in your product or service? What are their demographics, interests, and behaviors? You can use Instagram's built-in audience targeting tools to reach the right people.

2. Choose your ad format: Instagram offers several ad formats, including photo ads, video ads, carousel ads, and story ads. Choose the format that best suits your message and goals. For example, if you want to showcase multiple products, carousel ads might be a good choice.

3. Set your budget: Determine how much you're willing to spend on your Instagram ad campaign. You can choose a daily or lifetime budget, depending on your needs.

4. Create your ad: Use compelling visuals and copy to create an ad that will catch your target audience's attention. Make sure your ad is visually appealing and includes a clear call-to-action (CTA) that encourages people to take action, such as visiting your website or making a purchase.

5. Launch your campaign: Once you've created your ad, it's time to launch your campaign. You can use Instagram's Ads Manager to set up and launch your campaign.

6. Monitor and optimize your campaign: Keep an eye on your ad's performance and make adjustments as needed. Use Instagram's analytics tools to track metrics like reach, engagement, and conversions. Use this information to optimize your campaign and improve your results.

Here's an example of how a startup might run an Instagram ad campaign:

Let's say you're launching a new subscription box service that delivers healthy snacks to people's doors. Here's how you might run an Instagram ad campaign to promote your service:

- Define your target audience: Your target audience might be health-conscious millennials who are interested in trying new snacks and eating healthy.

- Choose your ad format: A carousel ad might be a good choice for showcasing the different snacks your subscription box includes.

- Set your budget: Let's say you're willing to spend $500 on your Instagram ad campaign.

- Create your ad: Use high-quality photos of your snacks and copy that emphasizes the convenience and health benefits of your subscription box. Include a clear CTA to sign up for your service.

- Launch your campaign: Use Instagram's Ads Manager to set up and launch your campaign, targeting health-conscious millennials.

- Monitor and optimize your campaign: Track metrics like reach, engagement, and conversions to see how your campaign is performing. Adjust your ad targeting or copy as needed to improve your results.

Google Ads

Google Ads is an advertising platform that allows businesses to create and display ads to potential customers when they search for relevant keywords or browse websites and apps that participate in Google's ad network. Here are the steps to get started with Google Ads:

1. Create a Google Ads account: You can sign up for a Google Ads account by visiting the Google Ads website and following the prompts to create an account.

2. Define your target audience: Before creating any ads, you need to define your target audience. This includes identifying the demographics, interests, and behaviors of your ideal customers.

3. Choose your keywords: Once you have defined your target audience, you can choose relevant keywords for your ads. These are the words or phrases that potential customers might search for when looking for your product or service.

4. Create your ads: With your target audience and keywords in mind, you can create your ads. These can be text, image, or video ads, and they should be designed to capture the attention of your target audience.

5. Set your budget: You will need to set a daily or monthly budget for your ads. You can choose to pay per click (PPC) or per impression (CPM), depending on your goals.

6. Launch your ads: Once you have created your ads and set your budget, you can launch your ads. Google will then display your ads to potential customers who meet your target audience and search for relevant keywords.

Example: Let's say you are a startup that sells eco-friendly cleaning products. You might define your target audience as environmentally conscious consumers who are interested in sustainable living. You could then choose keywords like "eco-friendly cleaning products" and "sustainable cleaning supplies" for your ads. Your ads could feature images of your products, along with messaging that emphasizes their eco-friendly benefits. You might set a budget of $500 per month and launch your ads on Google search results pages and websites that participate in the Google AdSense program.

Google Analytics

Google Analytics is a web analytics platform that allows businesses to track and analyze their website traffic. This can help startups understand how potential customers are finding and using their website, and identify areas for improvement. Here are the steps to get started with Google Analytics:

1. Create a Google Analytics account: You can sign up for a Google Analytics account by visiting the Google Analytics website and following the prompts to create an account.

2. Add the tracking code to your website: Once you have created your account, you will need to add the Google Analytics tracking code to your website. This will allow Google to track visitor behavior on your website.

3. Set up goals: You can set up goals in Google Analytics to track specific actions that visitors take on your website, such as making a purchase or filling out a contact form.

4. Analyze your data: With Google Analytics, you can analyze your website traffic to gain insights into how visitors are finding and using your website. This can help you make data-driven decisions about how to optimize your website for better performance.

Example: Let's say you are a startup that sells handmade jewelry online. You might use Google Analytics to track how visitors are finding your website, which pages are most popular, and how long visitors are staying on your site. You might set up a goal to track how many visitors make a purchase on your website, and use this data to optimize your product pages and checkout process for better conversion rates. You might also use Google Analytics to track how visitors are interacting with your social media channels, and adjust your social media strategy accordingly.

Linkedin Advertising

LinkedIn is a professional networking platform that provides a powerful advertising tool for businesses, particularly B2B startups. Here's a detailed guide on how to use LinkedIn advertising for a startup with some examples.

1. Define your target audience:

To get the most out of your LinkedIn advertising campaigns, it's essential to identify your target audience. Start by defining who your ideal customer is, including their job titles, industry, company size, and geographic location. LinkedIn offers a wide range of targeting options that allow you to reach your ideal audience.

Example: If you're a B2B SaaS startup that offers HR software, you could target HR managers, recruiters, and business owners in companies with over 100 employees in the United States.

2. Choose your ad format:

LinkedIn offers several ad formats to choose from, including sponsored content, sponsored InMail, display ads, and dynamic ads. The best ad format for your startup will depend on your campaign objective, target audience, and budget.

Example: If your objective is to generate leads for your HR software, sponsored content ads may be the best choice. You can create an engaging post with a clear call-to-action that directs users to your landing page.

3. Create your ad copy:

Your ad copy should be compelling, relevant to your target audience, and clearly convey the benefits of your product or service. Use clear and concise language that highlights your unique selling proposition (USP).

Example: If you're promoting an HR software that simplifies recruitment, your ad copy could say, "Say goodbye to manual recruitment processes. Our HR software makes hiring top talent faster and easier than ever."

4. Set your budget:

LinkedIn offers several bidding options, including cost-per-click (CPC), cost-per-impression (CPM), and cost-per-send (CPS). Set a budget that aligns with your campaign objectives and start with a smaller budget to test your ads' performance.

Example: If you have a budget of $1,000, you could start by running a sponsored content campaign with a $100 daily budget for ten days.

5. Track your performance:

Track your ad performance regularly to optimize your campaigns and achieve your objectives. LinkedIn offers a range of metrics that can help you measure your ad's effectiveness, including clicks, impressions, conversion rate, and cost per conversion.

Example: If you're running a sponsored content campaign, track the click-through rate (CTR) and the conversion rate. If you're not getting the desired results, try adjusting your targeting, ad copy, or budget.

In conclusion, LinkedIn advertising can be an effective way for startups to reach their target audience and achieve their business objectives.

Don'ts of Inorganic Marketing

While inorganic marketing can be effective in some cases, it can be costly and may not always provide the best return on investment for startups, especially those with limited resources. Here are some don'ts in inorganic marketing for startups:

- **Don't neglect your target audience:** It's important to ensure that your ads are being shown to the right people. If you don't target the right audience, you may end up wasting money on clicks or impressions from people who have no interest in your product or service. For example, if you sell high-end fashion products, you probably don't want to target people who are interested in discount shopping.

- **Don't overspend on ads:** While it's tempting to throw a lot of money into advertising, especially when you're just starting out, it's important to be strategic about your spending. Make sure you're getting a good return on investment (ROI) for your ads. For example, if you're spending

$100 on ads and only generating $50 in sales, you need to re-evaluate your ad strategy.

- **Don't rely solely on paid advertising:** Inorganic marketing should be just one part of your overall marketing strategy. It's important to also focus on organic marketing tactics like social media, content marketing, and SEO. These tactics can help you build a strong brand and generate leads without relying solely on paid advertising.

- **Don't ignore your analytics:** Make sure you're tracking the performance of your ads and adjusting your strategy as needed. Use analytics tools to track click-through rates, conversions, and other metrics. This will help you identify what's working and what's not, so you can make changes as needed.

- **Don't forget about your brand:** While inorganic marketing can be effective for getting your brand in front of more people, it's important to also focus on building a strong brand. Make sure your ads are consistent with your brand's messaging, tone, and visual identity.

Examples:

Let's say you're a startup that sells high-end athletic apparel for women. Here are some examples of "don'ts" of inorganic marketing:

-Don't target men: If you're running ads on Facebook, make sure you're targeting women who are interested in fitness and athletic apparel, rather than men who may have no interest in your products.

-Don't overspend on ads without tracking ROI: If you're running ads on Google AdWords, make sure you're tracking your conversion rates and adjusting your bids accordingly. If you're not getting a good ROI, consider pausing or adjusting your ads.

-Don't rely solely on paid advertising: While Google AdWords and Facebook ads can be effective, don't forget about other tactics like influencer marketing and content marketing.

-Don't ignore your analytics: Make sure you're using Google Analytics or other tools to track the performance of your ads, so you can identify what's working and what's not.

-Don't forget about your brand: Make sure your ads are consistent with your brand's messaging, tone, and visual identity. For example, if your brand is all about empowering women to be strong and confident, make sure your ads reflect that messaging.

By defining your target audience, choosing the right ad format, creating compelling ad copy, setting your budget, and tracking your performance, you can create successful campaigns that generate leads and drive revenue.

CHAPTER ELEVEN

Legal and Compliances

Adhering to legal requirements is crucial for any organization; knowledge and compliance with applicable laws is the initial step to ensure smooth business operations. Compliance with the relevant laws where the startup is doing business is important for the successful setup and efficient growth of startups. Compliance ensures that no penalty is imposed on a start-up at any point in its growth and helps it stay out of any other possible risks/ difficulties.

Starting a business in India involves various legal and compliance steps that a startup needs to follow.

Types of registered business entities

There are several types of registered business entities that a startup can choose from, depending on its needs and goals. Here are some of the most common types:

1. Sole Proprietorship: A sole proprietorship is a business owned and operated by one individual. It is the simplest form of business entity and does not require any formal registration. The owner is personally liable for all debts and obligations of the business. The benefits of a sole proprietorship include complete control over the business, minimal paperwork, and no corporate tax obligations. Examples of sole proprietorship include freelance writers, consultants, and small retail stores.

2. Partnership: A partnership is a business entity in which two or more people share ownership and control of the business. The partners share in the profits and losses of the business and are personally liable for its debts and obligations. There are two types of partnerships: general and limited. In a general partnership, all partners have unlimited liability for the business's debts and obligations. In a limited partnership, there is at least one general partner who is personally liable and at least one limited partner who is not. The benefits of a partnership include shared responsibilities and resources, minimal paperwork, and no corporate tax obligations. Examples of partnerships include law firms, accounting firms, and small retail businesses.

3. Limited Liability Company (LLC): An LLC is a hybrid business entity that combines the benefits of a corporation and a partnership. The owners of an LLC are called members, and they are not personally liable for the debts and obligations of the business. The LLC itself is responsible for paying taxes on its profits. The benefits of an LLC include limited liability, flexibility in management structure, and pass-through taxation. Examples of LLCs include real estate investment firms, online businesses, and professional service firms.

3. Corporation: A corporation is a legal entity that is separate from its owners. It can own property, enter into contracts, and sue or be sued. The owners of a corporation are called shareholders, and they are not personally liable for the debts and obligations of the business. The corporation pays taxes on its profits, and shareholders pay taxes on the dividends they receive. The benefits of a corporation include limited liability, the ability to raise capital by issuing stocks, and perpetual existence. Examples of corporations include multinational companies, tech startups, and manufacturing firms.

4. Cooperative: A cooperative is a business entity that is owned and controlled by its members, who share in the profits and decision-making. The members can be employees, customers, or suppliers. The benefits of a cooperative include shared resources and decision-making, democratic control, and tax advantages. Examples of cooperatives include credit unions, agricultural cooperatives, and worker cooperatives.

Choosing the right business entity for your startup is an important decision that will impact your legal and tax obligations, as well as your ability to raise capital and grow your business. It is advisable to consult with a lawyer or accountant before making a decision.

Registering the business entity

Registering a business entity for a startup in India can be a complex process, but it is crucial to do it right to establish a legal entity and avail the benefits of various schemes and incentives provided by the government. Here is a detailed guide on how to register a business entity for a startup in India:

1. **Choose the type of entity:** There are several types of business entities in India, including sole proprietorship, partnership, limited liability partnership (LLP), private limited company, and public limited company. Choose the type of entity based on the nature of your business, the number of founders, and the level of liability protection required.

2. **Obtain Digital Signature Certificate (DSC):** A DSC is required for filing various documents electronically, such as incorporation documents, annual returns, and tax returns. You can obtain a DSC from any certifying agency authorized by the Controller of Certifying Authorities.

3. **Obtain Director Identification Number (DIN):** If you are registering a private or public limited company, you need to obtain a DIN for all the proposed directors. You can apply for DIN online through the Ministry of Corporate Affairs (MCA) website.

4. **Apply for Name Approval:** The next step is to apply for name approval of your business entity. The name should be unique and should not resemble the name of any existing company. You can apply for name approval through the MCA website.

5. **Drafting of Memorandum of Association (MOA) and Articles of Association (AOA):** MOA and AOA are the legal documents that define the scope of activities and rules and regulations of the company. You need to draft these documents and get them printed on non judicial stamp paper.

6. **File Incorporation Documents:** Once the name is approved, and MOA and AOA are drafted, you can file the incorporation documents with the Registrar of Companies (ROC) online. The documents include Form SPICe, PAN and TAN application, MOA, AOA, and other supporting documents.

7. **Obtain Certificate of Incorporation:** If the ROC is satisfied with the documents, it will issue a Certificate of Incorporation. This document is proof of the existence of your company and includes the name, date of incorporation, and registration number of the company.

8. **Register for Goods and Services Tax (GST):** If your business is involved in the supply of goods or services, you need to register for GST. You can apply for GST registration online through the GST portal.

9. **Obtain Business Licenses and Permits:** Depending on the nature of your business, you may need to obtain various licenses and permits from the concerned authorities, such as FSSAI license for food-related

businesses, Shop and Establishment Act license, and Trade License.

10. **Open a Bank Account:** Once the company is incorporated, you need to open a bank account in the name of the company to carry out the financial transactions.

Examples:

Let's take an example of a startup that wants to register a private limited company in India.

- The founders decide to register a private limited company to avail of the benefits of limited liability protection and easy access to funding.
- They obtain a Digital Signature Certificate from a certifying agency authorized by the Controller of Certifying Authorities.
- They apply for Director Identification Number (DIN) for all the proposed directors online through the MCA website.
- They decide to name the company 'Tech Solutions Private Limited' and apply for name approval through the MCA website.
- They draft the Memorandum of Association (MOA) and Articles of Association (AOA) and get them printed on non-judicial stamp paper.
- They file the incorporation documents, including Form SPICe, PAN, and TAN application, MOA, AOA, and others

Obtaining necessary licenses and permits:

Starting a business requires various licenses and permits from government agencies at different levels. These licenses and permits may vary based on the type of business and its location. In general, there are a few common steps and examples to follow to obtain necessary licenses and permits for a startup.

Step 1: Determine the licenses and permits required for your business

The first step is to determine the licenses and permits required for your business. You can start by researching the licensing requirements on your state and local government websites, or you can contact the relevant government agencies for more information.

Some of the common licenses and permits required for most startups include:

- **Business license:** This license is required for almost all businesses and is issued by the city or county where the business operates.

- **Tax registration:** This permit is required to collect sales tax from customers and to pay taxes to the government.

- **Employer identification number (EIN):** This number is required if you have employees or plan to hire them. It is issued by the Internal Revenue Service (IRS).

- **Occupational license:** Some professions, such as lawyers, doctors, and accountants, require a professional license to practice.

- **Health department permits:** If your business involves food, health, or beauty products, you may need to obtain health department permits to comply with regulations.

- **Building permits:** If you plan to construct or renovate a building for your business, you may need building permits from the city or county.

Step 2: Complete the necessary paperwork and applications

Once you have identified the required licenses and permits, the next step is to complete the necessary paperwork and applications. The application process may vary based on the type of license or permit and the location of your business.

You will need to provide information such as your business name, location, type of business, number of employees, and other relevant details. You may also need to provide supporting documentation, such as proof of insurance, lease agreements, or zoning certificates.

Step 3: Submit the applications and pay the fees

After completing the paperwork and applications, you will need to submit them to the relevant government agencies along with the applicable fees. The fees may vary based on the type of license or permit and the location of your business.

Step 4: Wait for the approval

The approval process may take several weeks to several months depending on the type of license or permit and the location of your business. During this time, the government agencies may conduct inspections or request additional information or documentation.

Step 5: Receive the licenses and permits

Once the government agencies have approved your applications and received the fees, you will receive the necessary licenses and permits to start your business.

Examples of licenses and permits for a startup:

- If you are starting a restaurant, you may need to obtain health department permits for food preparation, sales tax permits, and building permits for construction or renovation.
- If you are starting a consulting business, you may need a professional license, business license, and tax registration.
- If you are starting a construction business, you may need a contractor's license, building permits, and tax registration.
- If you are starting a daycare center, you may need health department permits, background checks, and licensing from the state.
- It is important to research and obtain all the necessary licenses and permits before starting your business. Failure to do so can result in fines or even closure of your business.

Registering for taxes:

As a startup in India, it is important to register for various taxes to ensure compliance with the law. Here are some of the taxes that a startup may need to register for and the steps involved:

1. **Goods and Services Tax (GST) Registration:** Every business with an annual turnover of more than Rs. 40 lakhs (or Rs. 20 lakhs for some special category states) is required to register for GST.

Here are the steps to register for GST:

a. Visit the GST portal and create a username and password.

b. Fill out the GST registration form and submit the required documents, such as PAN card, Aadhaar card, bank account details, and business registration certificate.

c. After submitting the application, a GST officer will verify the details and issue a GST registration certificate.

2. **Permanent Account Number (PAN) Registration:** Every business is required to obtain a PAN card, which is a unique 10-digit alphanumeric

number issued by the Income Tax Department.

Here are the steps to register for PAN:

a. Visit the NSDL or UTIITSL website and fill out the PAN application form online.

b. Submit the required documents, such as identity proof, address proof, and business registration certificate.

c. Pay the registration fee and submit the application online.

d. After submitting the application, a PAN card will be issued within 15-20 working days.

3. **Tax Deduction and Collection Account Number (TAN) Registration:** If a business deducts tax at source or collects tax on behalf of the government, then it is required to obtain a TAN number.

Here are the steps to register for TAN:

a. Visit the NSDL website and fill out the TAN application form online.

b. Submit the required documents, such as PAN card and business registration certificate.

c. Pay the registration fee and submit the application online.

d. After submitting the application, a TAN number will be issued within 15-20 working days.

4. **Professional Tax Registration:** Professional tax is a state-level tax that is levied on professionals such as doctors, lawyers, and chartered accountants. The registration process varies from state to state, but generally involves submitting an application along with the required documents and paying the registration fee.

5. **Import Export Code (IEC) Registration:** If a business imports or exports goods or services, then it is required to obtain an IEC number.

Here are the steps to register for IEC:

a. Visit the DGFT website and fill out the IEC application form online.

b. Submit the required documents, such as PAN card, Aadhaar card, and bank account details.

c. Pay the registration fee and submit the application online.

d. After submitting the application, an IEC number will be issued within 2-3 working days.

Note that the registration process and requirements may vary depending on the type of business and the state in which it is registered. It is important to consult with a tax expert or visit the respective government websites for detailed information and guidance.

Drafting legal agreements

There are various types of legal agreements that a startup should consider drafting, depending on its business model and requirements. Below are some of the most common types of legal agreements a startup may need:

1. **Incorporation Documents:** These documents establish the legal entity of the startup and set out the rights and responsibilities of its shareholders. They typically include the company's Articles of Incorporation, Bylaws, and Shareholder Agreements.

2. **Articles of Incorporation:** This document sets out the basic information about the company, such as its name, purpose, and registered office. It also specifies the number and type of shares that can be issued, and the rights and privileges attached to each class of shares.

3. **Bylaws:** This document outlines the rules and procedures for running the company, including how meetings are conducted, how directors are appointed and removed, and how decisions are made.

4. **Shareholder Agreements:** This document governs the relationship between the shareholders and sets out the terms and conditions for the sale or transfer of shares. It also covers issues such as the payment of dividends, the appointment of directors, and the management of the company.

5. **Founders' Agreement:** This agreement sets out the terms of the relationship between the co-founders of the startup. It typically covers issues such as the ownership and division of equity, the roles and responsibilities of each founder, and how decisions are made.

6. **Non-Disclosure Agreement (NDA):** This agreement protects the confidential information of the startup by restricting the use and disclosure of such information by employees, contractors, or other parties who have access to it.

7. **Intellectual Property Assignment Agreement:** This agreement transfers the ownership of intellectual property rights (such as patents, trademarks, copyrights, and trade secrets) from the founders or employees to the startup.

8. **Employment Agreement:** This agreement sets out the terms and conditions of employment for employees, including their job duties, compensation, benefits, and termination rights.

9. **Service Agreement:** This agreement outlines the terms and conditions of the services to be provided by the startup to its clients or

customers.

Here are some samples of legal agreements:

Sample Articles of Incorporation: **https://www.sec.gov/about/forms/articlesinc.pdf**

Sample Bylaws: **https://www.nolo.com/legal-encyclopedia/sample-bylaws-corporation.html**

Sample Shareholder Agreement: **https://www.docracy.com/0e7xbp49y6/shareholders-agreement-template**

Sample Founders' Agreement: **https://www.docracy.com/2s0szuy8vi/founders-agreement-template**

Sample Non-Disclosure Agreement: **https://www.docracy.com/2hdh2w6ohm/non-disclosure-agreement-nda-template**

Sample Intellectual Property Assignment Agreement: **https://www.docracy.com/2h7qnk40p4/intellectual-property-assignment-agreement-template**

Sample Employment Agreement: **https://www.docracy.com/2xjkwxdgrw/employment-agreement-template**

Sample Service Agreement: **https://www.docracy.com/0xc8d88fom/service-agreement-template**

Please note that these samples are for informational purposes only and should not be used as a substitute for legal advice. It's important to consult with a qualified attorney to ensure that your startup's legal agreements are drafted and executed properly.

Types of legal agreements

There are various types of legal agreements that a startup in India should consider drafting, depending on its business model and requirements. Below are some of the most common types of legal agreements a startup may need:

1. Memorandum of Association (MoA) and Articles of Association (AoA): These documents establish the legal entity of the startup and set out the rights and responsibilities of its shareholders. They typically include the company's MoA, AoA, and Shareholder Agreements.

- MoA: This document sets out the basic information about the company, such as its name, purpose, and registered office. It also specifies the objects and powers of the company, and the liability of its members.

- AoA: This document outlines the rules and procedures for running the company, including how meetings are conducted, how directors are appointed and removed, and how decisions are made.

2. Shareholder Agreements: This document governs the relationship between the shareholders and sets out the terms and conditions for the sale or transfer of shares. It also covers issues such as the payment of dividends, the appointment of directors, and the management of the company.

3. Founders' Agreement: This agreement sets out the terms of the relationship between the co-founders of the startup. It typically covers issues such as the ownership and division of equity, the roles and responsibilities of each founder, and how decisions are made.

4. Non-Disclosure Agreement (NDA): This agreement protects the confidential information of the startup by restricting the use and disclosure of such information by employees, contractors, or other parties who have access to it.

5. Intellectual Property Assignment Agreement: This agreement transfers the ownership of intellectual property rights (such as patents, trademarks, copyrights, and trade secrets) from the founders or employees to the startup.

6. Employment Agreement: This agreement sets out the terms and conditions of employment for employees, including their job duties, compensation, benefits, and termination rights.

7. Service Agreement: This agreement outlines the terms and conditions of the services to be provided by the startup to its clients or customers.

Here are some examples and samples of legal agreements for startups in India:

Sample MoA and AoA: **https://www.mca.gov.in/content/dam/mca/ Ministry/pdf/ CompaniesincorporationThirdAmendmentRules_2019.pdf** (under the **Third Schedule**)

Sample Shareholder Agreement: **https://www.legalraasta.com/ shareholders-agreement-template/**

Sample Founders' Agreement: **https://www.legalraasta.com/founders- agreement-template/**

Sample Non-Disclosure Agreement: **https://www.legalraasta.com/ non-disclosure-agreement-nda/**

Sample Intellectual Property Assignment Agreement: **https://www.legalraasta.com/intellectual-property-assignment-agreement-template/**

Sample Employment Agreement: **https://www.legalraasta.com/employment-agreement/**

Sample Service Agreement: **https://www.legalraasta.com/service-agreement-template/**

Please note that these samples are for informational purposes only and should not be used as a substitute for legal advice. It's important to consult with a qualified attorney to ensure that your startup's legal agreements are drafted and executed properly under Indian laws.

Protecting intellectual property

Intellectual property (IP) refers to the intangible creations of the human mind, such as inventions, designs, literary and artistic works, symbols, and names used in commerce. Intellectual property is a critical aspect of a startup's success, as it protects the company's unique ideas, products, and services from competitors. In this chapter, we will discuss in detail the types of intellectual property, steps to protect intellectual property, and some examples.

Types of Intellectual Property

1. **Patents:** A patent is a legal document that grants the inventor the exclusive right to use, manufacture, and sell the invention for a specified period, usually 20 years. Patents are granted for inventions that are new, useful, and non-obvious. Some examples of patented inventions include the telephone, the airplane, and the computer mouse.

2. **Trademarks:** A trademark is a symbol, design, word, phrase, or combination that identifies and distinguishes a company's products or services from those of its competitors. Trademarks are registered with the government and typically last indefinitely as long as the trademark is in use. Examples of trademarks include the Nike "swoosh" logo and the Apple logo.

3. **Copyrights:** A copyright is a legal protection granted to the creator of an original work, such as a book, song, or software code. The creator has the exclusive right to reproduce, distribute, and perform the work for a specified period, usually the creator's lifetime plus 70 years. Examples of copyrighted works include books, music, and computer programs.

4. **Trade Secrets:** Trade secrets are confidential information that gives a company a competitive advantage. Trade secrets can include customer lists, manufacturing processes, and proprietary technology. Companies can protect trade secrets by requiring employees to sign non-disclosure agreements and implementing security measures to keep the information confidential.

Steps to Protect Intellectual Property

- **Conduct an IP Audit:** Startups should conduct an IP audit to identify and assess their intellectual property assets. The audit should include a review of patents, trademarks, copyrights, and trade secrets.

- **Register Patents, Trademarks, and Copyrights:** Startups should register their patents, trademarks, and copyrights with the government. This process involves submitting an application and paying a fee. Registration provides legal protection and makes it easier to enforce the company's rights.

- Use **Non-Disclosure Agreements (NDAs):** Startups should use NDAs to protect their trade secrets. NDAs are legal agreements that prohibit employees, contractors, and partners from disclosing confidential information.

-**Monitor and Enforce IP Rights:** Startups should monitor their IP rights to identify and stop infringement. This involves monitoring the market and filing lawsuits against infringers.

Examples of Intellectual Property:

- Amazon's One-Click Patent: Amazon's One-Click Patent is a patent that allows customers to make purchases with a single click. The patent has been the subject of controversy, as it has been used to prevent competitors from using similar technology.
- Apple's iPhone Trademark: Apple's iPhone trademark is one of the most recognizable trademarks in the world. The trademark has helped Apple establish itself as a leader in the smartphone market.
- Microsoft's Windows Copyright: Microsoft's Windows operating system is protected by copyright. The copyright prevents others from copying and distributing the software without permission.
- Coca-Cola's Trade Secret: Coca-Cola's secret formula for its soft drink is one of the most famous trade secrets in the world. The company has gone to great lengths to protect the formula, including keeping it in a vault and limiting the number of employees who have access to it.
-

In conclusion, startups should be aware of the different types of intellectual property, the steps to protect them, and some examples of successful IP strategies.

Complying with labor laws

Complying with labor laws is an essential requirement for any startup operating in India. It ensures that the rights of workers are protected, and the company operates within the legal framework. Here are some labor laws that startups in India should be aware of:

1. **The Minimum Wages Act, 1948:** This act regulates the minimum wages payable to employees in India. The minimum wage rates vary from state to state and are revised every few years. Startups need to ensure that they pay their employees at least the minimum wage rate prescribed by the state government.

Example: If a startup is located in Karnataka, they need to ensure that they pay their employees at least the minimum wage rate prescribed by the Karnataka government.

2. **The Employees' Provident Funds and Miscellaneous Provisions Act, 1952:** This act mandates employers to contribute to the Employee Provident Fund (EPF) of their employees. The contribution rate is currently 12% of the employee's basic salary and dearness allowance.

Example: If an employee's basic salary is Rs. 10,000, the employer needs to contribute Rs. 1,200 (12% of Rs. 10,000) to their EPF account.

3. **The Employees' State Insurance Act, 1948:** This act provides for the provision of medical benefits and insurance to employees. Employers need to contribute 4.75% of the employee's salary towards the Employees' State Insurance (ESI) scheme.

Example: If an employee's salary is Rs. 20,000, the employer needs to contribute Rs. 950 (4.75% of Rs. 20,000) towards their ESI scheme.

4. **The Payment of Bonus Act, 1965:** This act mandates employers to pay a bonus to their employees every year. The bonus amount should be at least 8.33% of the employee's salary or Rs. 100, whichever is higher.

Example: If an employee's salary is Rs. 15,000, the employer needs to pay them a bonus of at least Rs. 1,250 (8.33% of Rs. 15,000).

5. **The Payment of Gratuity Act, 1972:** This act mandates employers to pay gratuity to their employees on their retirement, resignation, or death. The gratuity amount should be at least 15 days' salary for every completed

year of service.

Example: If an employee has worked for a startup for 5 years and their last drawn salary was Rs. 20,000, the employer needs to pay them a gratuity of Rs. 15,000 (15 days' salary for every completed year of service, i.e., 5 years).

6. **The Maternity Benefit Act, 1961:** This act provides for paid maternity leave to female employees. Female employees are entitled to 26 weeks of paid maternity leave.

Example: If a female employee is eligible for maternity leave, the employer needs to provide them with 26 weeks of paid maternity leave.

7. **The Sexual Harassment of Women at Workplace (Prevention, Prohibition and Redressal) Act, 2013:** This act mandates employers to provide a safe and harassment-free workplace for female employees. Employers need to constitute an Internal Complaints Committee (ICC) to address complaints of sexual harassment.

Example: If a female employee files a complaint of sexual harassment, the employer needs to constitute an ICC to investigate the complaint and take necessary action.

Startups in India should ensure that they comply with all labor laws and regulations to avoid any legal issues and provide a safe and healthy workplace for their employees.

- A startup needs to comply with various labor laws such as minimum wage laws, working hours laws, and employment termination laws. Non-compliance with labor laws can result in legal action against the business.

Example: If you plan to hire employees, you need to comply with the minimum wage laws and ensure that the working hours are within the permissible limits.

Maintaining proper books of accounts

Maintaining proper books of accounts is crucial for any startup in India to ensure compliance with the law, prepare accurate financial statements, and make informed business decisions. Here are some important books of accounts that every startup in India should maintain:

1. **Cash book:** The cash book is used to record all transactions related to cash receipts and payments. It includes details such as date, amount, name of the party, and nature of the transaction.

Example: If a startup receives cash from a customer, it should be recorded in the cash book as a cash receipt along with the customer's name, date, and amount.

2. **Journal:** The journal is used to record transactions that do not involve cash, such as purchases on credit or sales on credit. It includes details such as date, name of the party, nature of the transaction, and the amount.

Example: If a startup purchases raw materials on credit from a supplier, it should be recorded in the journal as a credit purchase along with the supplier's name, date, and amount.

3. **Ledger:** The ledger is used to record transactions related to each account head, such as sales, purchases, and expenses. It includes details such as date, name of the party, nature of the transaction, and the amount.

Example: If a startup makes a payment to a vendor for office rent, it should be recorded in the ledger under the head of rent expenses along with the vendor's name, date, and amount.

4. **Sales register:** The sales register is used to record all sales made by the startup. It includes details such as date, name of the customer, nature of the transaction, and the amount.

Example: If a startup sells its product to a customer, it should be recorded in the sales register along with the customer's name, date, and amount.

5. **Purchase register:** The purchase register is used to record all purchases made by the startup. It includes details such as date, name of the vendor, nature of the transaction, and the amount.

Example: If a startup purchases raw materials from a vendor, it should be recorded in the purchase register along with the vendor's name, date, and amount.

6. **Bank book:** The bank book is used to record all transactions related to the bank account, such as deposits and withdrawals. It includes details such as date, name of the party, nature of the transaction, and the amount.

Example: If a startup receives a payment from a customer through a bank transfer, it should be recorded in the bank book along with the customer's name, date, and amount.

In addition to these books of accounts, startups in India should also maintain other important records such as invoices, bills, and receipts. It is essential to keep these records up to date and accurate to ensure compliance with the law and to make informed business decisions.

Conclusively, while there are many more regulations to comply with, some depending exclusively on the nature of your business, above mentioned are few important legal compliances that you must ensure in the initial days of setting up your startup. It is advisable to consult a lawyer or an accountant who can assist you in these processes accordingly.

CHAPTER TWELVE

How to pitch your idea

You've identified an underserved need and validated your startup idea. Now it's time to talk about your business—to potential clients, prospective customers, and future investors. Yet, how do you effectively communicate the promise of your idea and its possible impact on the market?

Pitching a business idea is one of the most nerve-wracking parts of any entrepreneur's journey. It's what stands in the way between your vision and the financing needed to turn that vision into reality. Although daunting, there are steps you can take to ensure a greater chance of success.

Here are some reasons why pitching is important, along with examples:

1. **Attracting investors:** Investors are always on the lookout for new business opportunities that can yield high returns. A well-crafted pitch can help entrepreneurs capture the attention of investors and persuade them to invest in their business. For example, when Elon Musk presented the idea of Tesla Motors to investors, he convinced them that the future of transportation lies in electric cars and that Tesla Motors is poised to become a leader in the industry. This led to significant investments in the company, which helped it grow into the successful business it is today.

2. **Winning clients:** Pitching is not just limited to investors; it is also crucial in winning clients. A persuasive pitch can help salespeople convince potential customers to buy their products or services. For example, when Steve Jobs launched the iPhone in 2007, he delivered a pitch that emphasized the device's innovative design, user interface, and features. This pitch helped Apple win millions of customers and establish the iPhone as one of the most popular smartphones in the world.

3. **Communicating ideas:** Pitching is also important in communicating ideas and proposals within an organization. A well-structured pitch can help professionals present their ideas to their colleagues or superiors and persuade them to support their initiatives. For example, when Sheryl

Sandberg presented the idea of creating a revenue model for Facebook, she convinced Mark Zuckerberg and other executives to adopt the model, which helped the company grow into a profitable business.

4. **Building relationships:** Finally, pitching is important in building relationships with investors, clients, and colleagues. A well-crafted pitch can help establish a connection with the audience and build trust and credibility. For example, when Richard Branson pitches his business ideas, he emphasizes the importance of creating a positive social impact and building a strong brand image. This approach has helped him build a loyal customer base and establish himself as a respected entrepreneur and philanthropist.

Pitching is a crucial skill that can help entrepreneurs, salespeople, and professionals succeed in their careers. By mastering the art of pitching, individuals can attract investors, win clients, communicate ideas, and build relationships.

How to pitch an idea?

Pitching an idea in a short amount of time requires you to be concise, clear, and compelling.

Here are some tips on how to do it, along with some examples:

1. **Start with a hook:** Begin your pitch with a hook that captures the listener's attention and makes them want to hear more. This can be a startling fact, a surprising statistic, or a personal anecdote.

For example:

Did you know that over 80% of small businesses fail within the first five years? Well, I've got an idea that could help change that.

As a busy working parent, I know how hard it can be to find time to cook healthy meals. That's why I've come up with a solution that could revolutionize the meal prep industry.

2. **Explain the problem:** Once you've hooked your listener, explain the problem that your idea solves. Be clear and specific about the issue, and use examples to help illustrate your point.

For example:

Small business owners often struggle to keep up with the demands of running a business while also managing their finances. This can lead to costly mistakes and ultimately, failure.

Many people want to eat healthy but don't have the time or expertise to plan and prepare meals. As a result, they end up eating unhealthy fast food or frozen dinners.

3. **Present your solution:** After you've outlined the problem, present your solution. Be clear and concise about what your idea is, how it works, and why it's different from other solutions out there. For example:

My idea is a simple, user-friendly app that helps small business owners track their finances and make informed decisions. It's affordable, easy to use, and customizable to each business's unique needs.

My solution is a meal prep service that delivers fresh, healthy meals to your door each week. Customers can choose from a variety of options and customize their meals to fit their dietary preferences and restrictions.

4. **Highlight the benefits:** Finally, emphasize the benefits of your idea. Explain how it can make a positive impact on people's lives, save them time or money, or solve a pressing issue.

For example:

With our app, small business owners can save time and money by streamlining their financial management. They'll have more time to focus on growing their business and less stress about their finances.

Our meal prep service makes it easy and convenient for people to eat healthy, even when they're busy. They'll have more energy, feel better, and be able to focus on the things that matter most to them.

Here are some more tips

-**Keep it brief:** Stick to the most important aspects of your idea and avoid getting bogged down in unnecessary details.

- **Focus on the benefits:** Emphasize the benefits of your idea, rather than just the features. This will help to make it more compelling to your audience.

Use examples: Where possible, use examples to illustrate your points and bring your idea to life.

- **Be clear and concise:** Use clear and concise language to make your pitch easy to understand.

Here is an example of how to pitch an idea in short and bullet points:
Idea: A mobile app that helps users to track their water intake

• Allows users to set daily water intake goals and track their progress

- Sends reminders throughout the day to encourage users to drink more water
- Provides personalized recommendations based on user data
- Offers a variety of water tracking options, including scanning barcodes on bottled water
- Includes a social sharing feature to help users stay motivated

Example: "Susan used our app to track her water intake and saw a 25% increase in hydration within two weeks."

Remember that a successful pitch is not just about the idea itself, but also about how you communicate it. Practice your pitch to refine your messaging and delivery, and be prepared to answer questions and engage in a dialogue with your audience. By following these steps, you can effectively pitch your idea and gain the support you need to turn it into a reality.

One Liner Pitch

A one liner pitch is a short and concise summary of a product, idea, or project that is delivered in a single sentence, with the aim of capturing the listener's attention and generating interest in what is being pitched.

Here are a few examples of one liner pitches with explanations:

- " The Netflix of education: access to thousands of online courses for a low monthly fee." This pitch is referring to an online learning platform that offers a wide range of courses, similar to how Netflix offers a wide range of TV shows and movies for a monthly fee.
- "The world's first smart water bottle that reminds you to stay hydrated and tracks your water intake." This pitch is referring to a water bottle that has technology built in to track how much water you drink and remind you to drink more, similar to how a fitness tracker might remind you to move more.
- "The Airbnb for camping: book unique camping experiences all over the world." This pitch is referring to a platform that allows people to rent out their land or unique camping experiences, similar to how Airbnb allows people to rent out their homes.
- "Tinder, but for dog adoption: swipe right to find your perfect furry match." This pitch is referring to a platform that connects people looking to adopt dogs with dogs available for adoption, using a swiping interface

similar to the popular dating app Tinder.

- "The ultimate meal prep tool: plan your meals, generate a shopping list, and track your macros all in one app." This pitch is referring to a meal planning and tracking app that helps people plan out their meals for the week, generate a shopping list, and track their macronutrient intake.

Elevator pitch

An elevator pitch is a brief, persuasive speech that summarizes a startup's business idea, products or services, and value proposition in a concise and compelling manner. It is called an elevator pitch because it is supposed to be short enough to be delivered during an elevator ride, usually lasting between 30 seconds to 2 minutes.

Here's an example of an elevator pitch for a startup:

"Hi, my name is John and I'm the founder of ABC Technologies. We've developed a revolutionary new app that helps people with diabetes manage their blood sugar levels more effectively. Our app uses artificial intelligence to analyze real-time data from continuous glucose monitors and provides personalized insights and recommendations to users, which can help them avoid dangerous highs and lows. We're currently in talks with several diabetes clinics and have already secured seed funding from a prominent VC firm. Our goal is to help millions of people with diabetes worldwide live healthier, more active lives."

In this example, the pitch clearly states the problem the startup is trying to solve (managing diabetes), the solution they've developed (an AI-powered app), the value proposition (personalized insights and recommendations), and their progress so far (partnerships and funding). It also includes a clear goal and vision for the company.

Sales pitch

A sales pitch is a persuasive speech or presentation aimed at convincing potential customers to buy a product or service. It typically highlights the benefits of the product or service and addresses the needs and pain points of the customer. Here are some examples of a sales pitch:

- Example 1:

Good afternoon, I'm Jane and I'm here to introduce you to our new fitness program. Are you tired of feeling sluggish and unhealthy? Our program is designed to help you lose weight, tone your body, and improve your overall health. We provide customized workout plans tailored to your specific goals and fitness level. Our trainers are certified professionals who will guide you every step of the way. With our program, you'll see results in just a few weeks. We offer a free trial session, so why not give us a try and see for yourself?

- Example 2:

Hello, my name is John and I'm here to tell you about our new software solution. Are you tired of spending hours on manual tasks? Our software can automate your workflow and save you time and money. It's easy to use and can be customized to meet your specific needs. With our software, you'll be able to streamline your operations and increase your productivity. We offer a free demo, so you can see how it works before you make a purchase. Try it out and take your business to the next level.

- Example 3:

Hi, my name is Sarah and I'm here to introduce you to our new line of skincare products. Do you struggle with acne or dry skin? Our products are specially formulated to address those issues and give you healthy, glowing skin. Our ingredients are all natural and free from harmful chemicals. Plus, our products are affordable and easy to use. With our skincare line, you can achieve the perfect complexion you've always wanted. Try it out and see the difference for yourself.

In all of these examples, the sales pitch addresses the needs and pain points of the customer and highlights the benefits of the product or service. It also offers a free trial or demo to encourage the customer to try it out before making a purchase.

Investment pitch

An investment pitch is a presentation made to potential investors to convince them to invest in a business or project. The goal of an investment pitch is to generate interest and secure funding for the proposed venture. It is typically delivered by entrepreneurs or business leaders to venture capitalists, angel investors, or other types of funding sources.

Here are some key elements that are typically included in an investment pitch:

1. **Executive Summary**: This is a brief overview of the proposed venture that highlights its key features, benefits, and potential for success.

2. **Problem Statement:** This section identifies the problem or challenge that the proposed venture aims to solve or address.

3. **Solution:** This is a detailed explanation of how the proposed venture will solve the identified problem or challenge.

4. **Market Analysis:** This section provides an analysis of the target market, including its size, growth potential, and competition.

5. **Marketing and Sales Strategy**: This section outlines the proposed marketing and sales strategy for the venture, including how it will reach and engage customers.

6. **Financial Projections**: This section provides financial projections for the proposed venture, including revenue, expenses, and profit margins.

7. **Investment Proposal:** This section outlines the specific investment opportunity being offered to potential investors, including the amount of funding being sought, the ownership structure, and the potential return on investment.

Examples of successful investment pitches include:

- Airbnb: In 2008, the founders of Airbnb created a pitch deck to secure funding for their startup. The pitch deck included slides that highlighted the problem of expensive hotels and the opportunity to rent out unused space in people's homes. The pitch deck helped Airbnb secure $600,000 in seed funding.
- Uber: In 2010, Uber's founders created a pitch deck to raise funding for their ride-hailing service. The pitch deck included slides that highlighted the problems with traditional taxis and the opportunity to create a more efficient and convenient transportation option. The pitch deck helped Uber secure $1.25 million in seed funding.
- Tesla: In 2004, Tesla's founders created a pitch deck to raise funding for their electric car company. The pitch deck included slides that highlighted the problems with traditional gasoline-powered cars and the opportunity to create a more sustainable and environmentally-friendly transportation option. The pitch deck helped Tesla secure $7.5 million in funding.

Overall, a successful investment pitch is one that clearly communicates the problem, solution, market opportunity, and financial projections in a compelling and persuasive manner.

Storytelling: An important skill for pitching

Storytelling is a powerful tool for effective pitching. It allows you to connect with your audience on an emotional level, engage them in your message, and create a memorable impression. Here are some reasons why storytelling is important for pitching:

1. Storytelling creates a personal connection: When you tell a story, you create a personal connection with your audience. You give them a glimpse into your personal experience or that of your customers or stakeholders. This personal connection helps build trust and credibility, making it easier for your audience to relate to your message.

2. Storytelling is memorable: People tend to remember stories more than facts and figures. When you tell a story, you create a visual and emotional image in the minds of your audience, making it more likely that they will remember your message long after your pitch is over.

3. Storytelling captures attention: Stories are inherently interesting and engaging. When you tell a story, you capture the attention of your audience and keep them engaged throughout your pitch. This can be particularly effective in a competitive pitching situation where you need to stand out from other presenters.

4. Storytelling helps simplify complex ideas: Often, the concepts or ideas you are pitching can be complex and difficult to understand. By using storytelling, you can simplify these ideas and make them more accessible to your audience.

Examples of effective storytelling in pitching:

- The Airbnb Story: Airbnb used storytelling to explain their concept of "belonging anywhere." The founders shared the story of their first guest, who was a woman who needed a place to stay during a design conference. She couldn't afford a hotel room, so they offered her an air mattress in their living room. This experience inspired them to create a platform where anyone could find a place to stay, no matter their budget. This personal story helped investors and customers understand the emotional appeal of the Airbnb platform.

- The Dollar Shave Club Story: Dollar Shave Club used storytelling to differentiate themselves from other razor companies. Their founder filmed a humorous video introducing the company and explaining why they were different. The video went viral, and the company quickly gained a large following. This story helped investors and customers understand the company's unique selling proposition and helped them stand out in a crowded market.

Importance of Storyline

A storyline in a startup pitch is a narrative or flow that describes the founding story, mission, and goals of the startup. It is the way founders present their company to investors, customers, and other stakeholders to explain why their idea is unique, valuable, and worth investing in.

The storyline typically includes the following elements:

- **The problem:** A clear description of the problem the startup is trying to solve, why it matters, and how big the market opportunity is.

- **The solution:** A description of the startup's product or service and how it addresses the problem in a unique and innovative way.

- **The market:** An analysis of the target market, including size, growth potential, and competition.

- **The team:** A brief overview of the founding team's background and experience, highlighting relevant skills and accomplishments.

- **The traction:** Evidence of early traction or validation, such as customer testimonials, revenue growth, or partnerships.

- **The ask:** A clear and concise request for investment, partnership, or support.

By presenting a compelling and well-crafted storyline, founders can help investors and stakeholders understand the value and potential of their startup and increase the chances of securing funding and support.

Introduction

The introduction of a storyline is critical to capturing and maintaining the audience's attention. It sets the stage for the rest of the pitch and creates a sense of intrigue and anticipation for what's to come.

A powerful introduction should hook the listener from the very beginning, whether it's through a thought-provoking question, a surprising statistic, a compelling anecdote, or a vivid description. It should also establish the main problem or challenge that the pitch is addressing, and make the audience feel the urgency and relevance of the topic.

Furthermore, a well-crafted introduction can also help establish credibility and trust with the audience by demonstrating the speaker's knowledge, experience, and passion for the subject matter. It can also help establish a connection with the audience by appealing to their emotions and values.

In short, a strong introduction is essential to crafting a great pitch that resonates with the audience and inspires action.

Pitch Deck

A pitch deck is a visual presentation that provides an overview of your startup to potential investors, partners, or customers. The purpose of a pitch deck is to grab the audience's attention and persuade them to take a specific action, such as investing in your business, partnering with you, or purchasing your product.

Here is a general outline of the format of a pitch deck:

1. **Cover Slide:** This slide should include your startup's name, logo, and a tagline that briefly summarizes your company.

2. **Problem Statement:** Describe the problem your startup solves, and explain why it's important.

3. **Solution:** Explain your startup's solution to the problem, and how it is unique compared to other solutions.

4. **Market Size and Opportunity:** Describe the size of your market, your target audience, and how your solution fits into the market.

5. **Business Model:** Explain how your startup generates revenue, and provide projections for future growth.

6. **Marketing and Sales Strategy:** Describe how you plan to market and sell your product or service.

7. **Competitive Analysis:** Provide an overview of your competition and explain how your startup is different.

8. **Team:** Introduce your startup's founders and key team members, and explain their relevant experience.

9. **Financials:** Provide financial projections for your startup, including revenue, expenses, and profit margins.

10. **Ask:** Close your pitch deck with a clear ask, such as a funding request, partnership proposal, or customer acquisition plan.

It's important to keep your pitch deck concise and visually appealing, using graphics and images to supplement your key points. The length of your pitch deck may vary, but it should typically be around 10-15 slides. Remember to practice your pitch and be prepared to answer questions from your audience.

Do's and Don'ts of pitching

Several entrepreneurs in India find themselves clueless when it comes to the art of pitching a business idea to an investor. Some feel hesitant on approaching an external party for money while others don't trust partnering a VC or angel investor fearing loss of control.

Pitching is an important skill that can make or break your business or project. Here are some dos and don'ts to keep in mind when pitching:

Dos:

- Be prepared: Know your audience, research their interests and be ready to answer any questions they may have.

- Keep it concise: A good pitch should be clear, concise and to the point. Avoid rambling or getting bogged down in details.

- Focus on benefits: Highlight the benefits of your product or idea, and how it can solve a problem or meet a need.

- Use visuals: Visual aids like graphs, charts or product demos can help to illustrate your points and make your pitch more engaging.

- Be confident: Show confidence in yourself and your idea. Speak clearly and with conviction.

- Practice, practice, practice: Practice your pitch until you can deliver it flawlessly, even under pressure.

Don'ts:

- Don't be vague: Your pitch should be specific and clearly define your product or idea.

- Don't oversell: While it's important to highlight the benefits of your product, don't oversell it or make promises you can't keep.

- Don't forget the competition: Be aware of your competition and how your product or idea compares to theirs.

- Don't be too technical: Avoid using jargon or technical language that your audience may not understand.

- Don't be unprepared: Make sure you have all the materials and equipment you need for your pitch.

- Don't be defensive: Be open to feedback and don't get defensive if your audience has questions or concerns about your idea.

What investors look for in a pitch?

Investors typically look for several key factors when evaluating a startup pitch:

1. **Problem and Solution:** The investor wants to understand what problem the startup is solving and how their solution is unique and innovative compared to other solutions in the market.

2. **Market Size and Potential:** Investors want to see that there is a significant market opportunity for the startup's solution and that the market is growing or has the potential to grow.

3. **Business Model:** Investors want to understand the startup's business model and how it plans to make money. This includes revenue streams, pricing strategy, customer acquisition, and growth plans.

4. **Team:** Investors want to see a strong and capable team with relevant experience and expertise. This includes the founder's vision and passion for

the startup, as well as their ability to execute and scale the business.

5. Traction: Investors want to see evidence that the startup has made progress and achieved some level of traction. This includes user adoption, revenue growth, partnerships, and other milestones.

6. Competitive Advantage: Investors want to understand the startup's competitive advantage and how it plans to stay ahead of competitors in the market.

7. Exit Strategy: Finally, investors want to understand the startup's long-term plan and how they plan to create value for investors. This includes a clear exit strategy, such as acquisition or IPO.

In addition, by creating a personal connection, making your message memorable, capturing attention, and simplifying complex ideas, storytelling in the pitch deck can help you deliver a pitch that resonates with your audience and achieves your goals.

"In the modern world of business it is useless to be a creative, original thinker unless you can sell what you create. Management can not be expected to recognize a good idea unless it is presented to them by a good salesman." – David Ogilvy